GUY gets GIRL GIRL gets GUY

Larry GLANZ
Robert H. PHILLIPS

SQUAREONE
PUBLISHERS

COVER DESIGNER: Phaedra Mastrocola
IN-HOUSE EDITOR: Helene Ciaravino
TYPESETTER: Gary A. Rosenberg

Square One Publishers
115 Herricks Road
Garden City Park, NY 11040
877-900-BOOK
www.squareonepublishers.com

Library of Congress Cataloging-in-Publication Data

Glanz, Larry.
  Guy gets girl girl gets guy : where to go to find romance & what to
say when you find it / Larry Glanz and Robert H. Phillips.
    p. cm.
  Includes index.
  ISBN 0-7570-0126-2 (pbk.)
  1. Dating (Social customs) 2. Man-woman relationships.
3. Conversation. I. Phillips, Robert H., 1948– II. Title.
HQ801 .G513   2004
646.7'7—dc22

                                                          2003024082

Printed in the United States of America

10   9   8   7   6   5   4   3   2   1

Contents

To my mother, to whom I owe it all.

To my dear departed dad,
whose spirit lives on within me.

To my late grandfather Sam Spitalny,
who provided the inspiration for my profession.

To my sister Barbara, and nieces Wendy and Lisa,
of whom I am incredibly proud.

Special thanks to my step-dad Harry,
and my nephews-in-law Michael and Eric,
who are absolutely the best.

To Kim, my soulmate, lifemate
and main squeeze through eternity.

To my wonderful boys Tom, Tam, and Thu.

To my posse, Noble, Edgar, and Allen,
who brighten up my life.

L.G.

To my wife, Sharon, and my sons,
Michael, Larry, and Steven, who provide the nucleus.

To my parents and sister,
who provided the foundation.

To my late grandparents,
who provided the inspiration.

And to the rest of my family, in-laws, and friends,
who provide the icing on the cake.

R.H.P.

Acknowledgments

I would like to thank all of the people I have met who have encouraged me to write this book.

And a very special thank you to the following people for their invaluable input into the making of this book: Michael Laurence, Ray Slawecki, Dave Rumsey, Harry Zabarkes, Eric Spinner, Craig Trude, Tim Bauman, Bob Junas, Jim Wilk, Jeff Jorczak, Marybeth Appert, Maureen Richardson, John Shaw, Trish McDermott, Bridgette A. Cush, Wendy Zocks, Dale Winchell and Robert Kavanaugh.

And an extra special thank you to Rudy Shur, publisher extraordinaire.

L.G.

In addition to the people mentioned above, I would like to thank the members of my staff—Melissa Sheinwold, Carmela Vecchio, Donna Storan, and Ann Dominger—who were instrumental in the prompt and efficient preparation of the drafts and final copy of this manuscript.

R.H.P.

A Note on Gender Usage

To avoid long and awkward phrasing within sentences, the publisher has chosen to alternate the use of male and female pronouns according to chapter. Therefore, when referring to potential prospects, odd-numbered chapters use female pronouns, while even-numbered chapters employ male pronouns, to give acknowledgment to both genders. Please realize that no offense or slight is intended.

Introduction

Success in attaining your goals in life begins with knowledge. Congratulations! By obtaining this book, you have taken an important step. You have selected a source that will help you gain essential knowledge and enable you to reach a specific goal—namely, to meet and win the person with whom you desire to spend your days, evenings, and possibly the rest of your life.

Essentially, this book is for any man or woman who is seeking a relationship to enhance life and end loneliness. It is for singles of any age who want to improve their confidence and skills for meeting people. In this book, we have taken a serious, practical, but lighthearted look at the "wheres" and "how tos" of locating and attracting someone special. Maybe you already have someone in mind— that adorable guy who lives in the apartment above you; that stunning girl you've been noticing on the treadmill at the gym. Or maybe you are still scouting for your perfect match and need a few ideas on where to find that person. Either way, this book can help.

The directions, techniques, and philosophies that follow have been tried time and time again, with amazingly successful results. Read the book several times if necessary, until you feel comfortable enough to apply the advice that is suitable for your particular situation. Then use the newfound knowledge to find that special someone.

Chances are you wouldn't be reading this book unless you felt you had a few weak points when it comes to meeting and dating others. Aim to become adept at implementing at least some of the strategies found within this book's covers. Remember, it will take an open mind and lots of positive energy on your part to put your new knowledge successfully to work.

You want a fresh start, so create a fresh new you! We'll begin by guiding you through a little self-analysis. What needs changing? What needs bolstering? Then we'll cover where to go and what to say. You will have plenty of starting points by the time you finish this guidebook.

The singles scene today can be *scary*! We want to help you enjoy it and meet some wonderful people in the process. So how do you go about joining the couples scene? Read on.

PART ONE

How to Meet Someone Special

*P*laying single is not easy when your heart is set on a game for two. You probably feel disillusioned: "Is there *anyone* for me out there?" You may even have started to question yourself: "Is it what I'm wearing?" "Do I sound unintelligent?" Before we go any further, realize there is nothing fundamentally wrong with you just because you are still looking for someone special. You simply may not have developed your dating craft to the point where it is working optimally for you. Part I will walk you through how to do so.

You are a commodity, and you can be a *hot* commodity at that. So we begin with a few marketing strategies. Think of yourself as a product to be attractively packaged and carefully advertised. Part I gives you helpful hints on how to accentuate your assets, be prepared for chance meetings, and pursue good opportunities. We will discuss how to choose prospects, keep track of the good ones, and start effective conversations. You will find helpful icebreakers and even winning techniques that will make you savvy on the singles scene.

1

Making the Most of Your Product

*G*irls, have you ever walked though a shopping mall or gone out to dinner with friends and spotted a handsome, well-dressed man with a not-so-attractive woman? Haven't you wondered what *she* has that helped her find such a man? You might have thought, "She must work for him, because he could do so much better. He could have *me*!"

Guys, when at a sporting event or dance club, have you ever noticed an absolute knockout of a woman with a geeky guy? Haven't you asked yourself, "What does *he* have that got him such a beauty? He must be rich because there is no way on earth that she could be interested in a guy like him—not when *I'm* available."

Well, beauty is indeed in the eye of the beholder. But if you are perplexed, questioning why *you* are not the one with that gorgeous guy or glamorous girl, then you might want to begin by taking stock of your own strengths and weaknesses. Ask yourself: What type of appearance do I make? How do others perceive me? Do I have stylish clothes? Am I clean and well groomed? Do I have a positive attitude? Do I really believe I am capable of meeting someone who wants me and will accept me, regardless of my faults? Is it worth putting forth a great effort to improve myself in order to meet someone nice? How badly do I want someone special in my life? Am I reading this book out of curiosity, or do I really mean business?

Take stock of who you are. List your strong points (don't be modest, now) as well as your weak points (be constructive). Identify the areas you'd like to improve and then start making changes! Update that wardrobe, start lifting weights again, brush up on your knowledge of current events—whatever you need to do in order to bolster your confidence and make yourself more desirable. Some of the most common areas targeted for self-improvement revolve around appearance, manners, habits, and attitude. Let's discuss these in more detail.

MAXIMIZE YOUR APPEARANCE

Some people are fortunate enough to be really good-looking. Others have to work harder at their appearance and maximize their best features. Take the time to assess your physical appearance. Learn how to show off your strong points and diminish your weak points.

Making the most of the looks you were born with is a lot like playing gin rummy. In the card game, you can improve the hand you're dealt by selecting other cards. If you make the correct selections, you can win the game. The same principle applies to your appearance. If you put forth enough effort, you can improve what you look like. This can result in increased success in finding that someone special and winning at the age-old game of love.

Think of yourself as a product. A large part of what makes a person try a product is that product's packaging. Now, how marketable are you? Do you have attention-getting packaging? Does this packaging reflect who you really are? Does it present you in the best possible way? If the answer to any of these questions is no, or you're not sure, then you have found an area that needs improvement! You, in essence, must make yourself as desirable as possible to potential prospects.

Okay, so you can't judge a book by its cover. But let's face it, the cover has to be sufficiently interesting in order for someone to want to open the book in the first place! If you're single and searching for a mate but convey a lackluster appearance, then you'll certainly want to start by concentrating your efforts on whipping your appearance into its most marketable shape.

So take stock. And be brutally honest. Which areas of your physical appearance could use some improvement? Consider your skin, smile, teeth, eyes, hair—all the areas that can give either an inviting or discouraging first impression. You may not always focus on problems in these areas, but rest assured your prospects will!

Clothing is also important to consider. Dressing for success is a key factor in practically all facets of life. Do you want to be successful in your efforts to meet someone? Then clean, well-kept, stylish clothes and shoes are a must. When was the last time you upgraded your wardrobe? Check it out now and make the necessary changes.

First impressions are critically important. Your appearance can make the difference when making contact with someone. No matter how bright, clever, entertaining, warm, talented, and delightful you are, few people will bother to notice these attributes if your exterior doesn't motivate them to stick around and discover it all. The experts agree: Make the most of your physical features and how you accessorize them. It should be the first phase of your self-promotion campaign.

POLISH YOUR TABLE MANNERS

Table manners count, too. This is an area in which many people didn't receive proper guidance as children. Subsequently, they have grown into adults without a clue as to how to act and eat at the table. Poor manners can definitely be a turnoff. Which poor table manners are most offensive? Speaking while you have food in your mouth, smacking your lips, slurping, belching, neglecting excess food on your face and teeth, and holding utensils as though they are small shovels are just a few unappetizing examples.

You may look great, but crummy table manners can kill those good looks. If you're not sure whether or not your manners are up to snuff, seek out a book on proper etiquette at the library or ask someone whom you trust and know will be honest.

Remember, the singles scene often involves dining in restaurants. So this part of your presentation is crucial to your success.

ELIMINATE BAD HABITS

There are many bad habits that can doom a new relationship. No, we're not just talking about addictions to drugs and alcohol—which can certainly doom you, too. There are other addictions or habits that can have a negative impact on your efforts, as well.

Smoking

Do you smoke cigarettes, cigars, or pipes? If the answer is yes, it might be smart to refrain from smoking in the presence of a nonsmoker. As many nonsmokers simply refuse to date smokers, exercising control of this habit could expand your list of dating prospects. Better yet, maybe your determination to meet someone special will give you the courage and motivation to quit smoking altogether!

What are the benefits of quitting? You will eliminate the offensive smell of smoke on your breath, hair, and clothing; add years to your life; and save a substantial amount of money on tobacco products and possibly medical bills!

Yawning

Yawning gives the distinct impression that you are bored, disinterested, or tired. You don't want to be thought of in that way, do you? No one wants to date someone who appears emotionally aloof or physically exhausted.

Some people, merely out of habit, yawn even when they are not tired. If you are one of these people, make a conscious effort to keep from performing this "act of boredom" when you're out with someone. Being mentally aware of your tendency to yawn will help you to control your habit. At the very least, you should try to cover up the yawn or make it less noticeable.

If you yawn because you are truly in need of sleep, then it is probably best to call it a night and get to bed. But for any future dates or plans you might have, be sure you get a good rest the night before. The day of the date, try to catch some zzz's after work or school to recharge your body. After all, a well-rested, enthusiastic person is a fun person to go out with.

Staring

Making eye contact is always good; it can be sexy, playful, and bold. But staring is another story. It is a habit that can certainly frighten away prospects. Staring can be too intense and aggressive, making a person wary of you. If you tend to stare at people whom you find attractive and interesting, you are probably asserting yourself too much.

Furthermore, if you are on a date, staring at someone else can be a supreme insult to the person you are with. When you are in the company of someone you like or to whom you are attracted, always give 100 percent of your attention to that person. Make eye contact with your date. Undivided attention will help generate chemistry between the two of you.

The list could go on and on. Do you use foul language, bite your fingernails, or crack your knuckles? These are not positive attributes, and they can be detrimental in attracting prospective partners. What can you do about these and other bad habits? Begin by making a list of your negative attributes (don't be embarrassed—you're helping yourself achieve a goal!), then put the list in a prominent place where you can review it often. Monitor your progress in controlling or eliminating these habits. All it takes is a dedicated, conscientious effort on your part to get yourself on the right track. Once you have all or most of these negative habits under control, not only will you be a better person for your efforts, but you will increase the likelihood of success in meeting someone special.

IMPROVE YOUR ATTITUDE

You've already started to work on your physical appearance and behavior. Now it's time to go to work on your mental frame of mind. Getting your mental attitude synchronized with your physical being is very important. In fact, a positive attitude can make all the difference.

If you are absolutely serious about your mission, you must always maintain a positive frame of mind. For your effort and commitment, hopefully, you will be rewarded with true love. Sure, it can be very depressing, frustrating, and expensive to pursue opportunities to meet someone special. Nevertheless, the end result of finding love and ending your loneliness is well worth whatever effort is required.

First, let's work on motivation and optimism. Keep the following thoughts in mind:

- You really want someone in your life *now*, not sometime in the next ten years.

- That special someone is out there waiting to meet you.

- That person *can* become attracted to you.

- It is worth putting forth any effort to meet that special person.

Now, how about the attitude you show to others? It may need some fine-tuning. Are you a happy and even-tempered person, or do you often act like you woke up and had a bowl of tacks for breakfast? It is a very important part of your self-promotion program to make a conscious effort to be the nicest person you can possibly be. Be caring, polite, respectful, and thoughtful. Most importantly, be sincere. Treat others the way you want to be treated, without expecting to get something in return.

Rid yourself of any bitterness, anger, or belligerence that may have resulted from previous bad relationships or marriages. If this is a serious problem, consider therapy. Professional counseling can help you resolve hostilities and other mental attitude problems. Remember, the next person you meet is *not* responsible for the "tortures" of your past. While you may have every right to be angry or bitter, do you have the right to transfer those feelings to a new person? Of course not. And this new person might be just what you need to be happy again. So why jeopardize a good opportunity by lugging around and displaying old baggage?

A hostile attitude can be a real turnoff to a potential prospect. Anyone with common sense will avoid you like the plague the moment your negative attitude surfaces. Go with the odds. It is more likely that someone special will discover and fall in love with a genuinely nice, positive person than a negatively charged one.

PRACTICE FLEXIBILITY

Are you willing to change your behavior patterns? As you get older, you may become more set in your ways, making you less flexible than you once were. It is always important to be flexible in your thinking. Be willing to make compromises. The person you desire may have firm beliefs in a particular area, and if you have the capacity to "go with the flow," it may help make a long-term relationship possible.

The following example illustrates how the ability to be flexible can enhance an existing relationship. Joe was a classic rock-and-roll junkie, while Mary enjoyed country music. That was fine when they listened to their own radios, but when they were together, they compromised on jazz and soft rock. Every now and then, together they would listen to rock-and-roll or country music. Guess what? Joe found that he actually started to like some of the songs Mary liked, and vice versa. Fortunately, they were both flexible and willing to compromise. That's the key.

The issue of flexibility can encompass many different areas—foods, movies, sports, hobbies, and so on. It is an important ingredient in a successful relationship.

CHANNEL YOUR WILLPOWER

Let's review. Can you honestly say your attitude is good? Your disposition in control? Your less-attractive habits in check? Your appearance better than ever? Great. Now it's time to address the next item—willpower. This is the time to exercise your "stick-to-it-ness." It does take energy, but if you give up on your goal, the odds of meeting the right person will be significantly reduced.

This book advocates an active but low-key approach to meeting and attracting a potential partner. Chance is not enough. You need to develop the willpower to improve all aspects of your personal being and to persist at your search.

Remember, your main source of strength is your inner self. How much do you want to improve your life? Dig down into that inner strength and make it happen. You have the willpower to find success!

VERBALLY EXPRESS YOURSELF

Human beings are as unique as snowflakes. Each person reacts differently in social situations, and each person displays or hides her reactions in her own way. Positive and negative feelings develop all the time. The tough part is that we cannot always understand the nuances in each other's emotions. That's why we need to talk to one another in a productive way.

It is the ability to verbally communicate your innermost thoughts and feelings that helps you effectively create and advance healthy interpersonal relationships. What if your thoughts and feelings remain unexplored and unexpressed? Unfortunately, you won't be doing much to enhance the future of the relationship. In addition, medical studies have found that people who hold back their feelings and keep them bottled up are at an increased risk for many debilitating illnesses.

Strive to be open and honest with the feelings you have in your heart and mind, and express them through carefully chosen words. Through this communication, you can create a more solid bond with your prospect, gain more respect and loyalty for your honesty and openness, and maintain a healthier physical and emotional state.

LEARN ACCEPTANCE

Be encouraged, not discouraged. Accept the fact that not every potential prospect will be attracted to you or respond to you in a positive way. But by doing your best to be friendly, polite, and sincere, you are certainly multiplying your chances of meeting someone truly special.

The techniques in this book won't work with every person you encounter, and some rejection is a natural part of the process. But it is important to realize that people are not really rejecting you—they don't even know you! They're rejecting what they think they know. And it's their loss. It is important for you to accept a rejection gracefully without becoming hostile or feeling unreasonably hurt.

Any time you encounter a person who is not interested in you, tell yourself that there are plenty of others who will be interested once they get to know you. Do not become discouraged and do not let your attitude sour. Keep working at it—the results are worth it!

A WORD TO THE WISE

How do you know when to continue pursuing a prospect? Look for signs such as eye contact, a smile, and positive body language—a lean in your direction or an open-facing stance, for example. Listen carefully for verbal clues that tell you to continue the conversation. If these signals stop or don't exist, chances are there may be no current interest on the prospect's part. If your instincts lead you to believe that the pursuit will be unproductive, gather your positive energy and move on to someone new.

2

Developing a List of Prospects

*B*asically, there are two categories of prospects—ones you will, in all probability, meet only once, and others whom you will encounter a number of times. For the "one-shot" encounters, your unexpected meeting may be your "only chance to dance." You'll need to quickly break the ice, get a conversation started, then close the deal. There is no way to list such prospects in advance and gather information on them for the next meeting. But you can use the skills you acquire in the following chapters to be desirable, approachable, interesting, and relatable during those wonderful chance meetings.

Then there are the prospects whom you are likely to come into contact with on more than one occasion—people who work in local stores, neighbors, close friends of family members, classmates, and work acquaintances, just to name a few. This chapter will help you develop and maintain a list of such prospects. The list will be a valuable source of information.

CREATING THE LIST

Your key to developing a successful list is to always record your prospects' names, as well as any interesting details about them. Any time you meet a prospective love interest, immediately jot down his name, along with when, how, and where you met. List any observations—be a sharp detective—and include even seemingly insignificant details that you can recall from the encounter. Record this data on a card or notepad that you keep in your wallet or pocketbook.

In the sales field, this technique is called "prospecting." Potential new accounts or customer leads are logged onto account-information cards where prospects' names and pertinent information are stored. The wealth of information that is accumulated on these cards helps people in the sales field convert leads into accounts or customers. It helps sales-people hone in on a prospect's "hot buttons." These buttons must first be targeted, then pushed in order for the sale to be made. A sales-person's success rate is reliant upon how skilled he is at identifying these buttons. The information on *your* cards should help you convert prospects into dates and, hopefully, arrive at that successful relation-ship. Use this information to target your prospects' hot buttons.

It's a good idea to periodically review your list. The next time you encounter one of your prospects—whether by chance or through "plan-ning"—you will be able to remember the person's name and a few bits of pertinent information. This knowledge can be a welcome icebreaker during an encounter.

PUTTING THEORY INTO PRACTICE

Is making a list of possible love interests actually worth the effort? How can your prospect list help you in your search? To illustrate, let's take a look at Sue's list:

Tom — Works at stationery store, Lakers fan, met on Saturday at 2:30 PM.

Jack — Neighbor in adjoining apartment complex, fireman, has German Shepherd named "Brutus," met on Tuesday 10:30 PM while he was walking dog.

Bill — Met on Monday at 9:00 AM at the local 7-11 (he was getting coffee), owns construction company.

Now, let's see how Sue used the information on her list to press one of Tom's hot buttons. Sue wasn't really a sports fan, let alone a basket-ball fan, but the first time she met Tom she figured that he liked the Los Angeles Lakers because he was wearing a Lakers cap. So, for the entire next week, she scanned the sports pages to see how the Lakers were doing. It just so happened that on Thursday night of that week, the Lak-ers won a double-overtime thriller against the New York Knicks on a last-second buzzer beater. Armed with this information, Sue went to the stationery store at about 2:30 the following Saturday afternoon, "prospecting" for Tom under the guise of seeking stationery supplies. Their conversation went like this:

Sue: Hi, Tom. How've you been?

Tom: Oh, I'm fine.

Sue: You should be more than fine. You should be in heaven after that double-overtime Lakers win over the Knicks on Thursday.

Tom: That was such a great game! I'm sorry, I forgot your name.

Sue: Sue.

Tom: I'm not very good with names. Are you a Lakers fan, Sue?

Sue: I'm starting to become one.

Tom: A Lakers game is an experience for me. I'm a diehard fan.

Sue: I've never been to a Lakers game, but I'd love to go to one.

Tom: Well, if you'd like, maybe I could take you to one.

Sue: That would be nice.

Tom: I have to get back to work here. Why don't you give me your number so I can call you to make plans. I'll check my Lakers schedule when I get home.

This example shows the importance of keeping prospect information. Sue knew the day and time Tom was likely to be working. She was prepared to speak with Tom about the Lakers, which was, in fact, one of his hot buttons.

There is an old saying: "He who fails to plan, plans to fail." Sue put considerable planning and preparation into developing a possible conversation with Tom. And that is what moved the odds for success in her favor. If Sue had not remembered or taken note of Tom's name and his interest in the Lakers, he might not have taken the time to make small talk with her. But because Sue was prepared, she caught Tom off guard and commanded his attention and interest.

Knowing even a little information about a prospect will help you make a connection. Simply remembering the name and anything significant about the person will garner immediate attention.

Interested in another example? Let's take a look at John's list:

Mandy — Lottery-ticket cashier at drugstore, loves jazz, met on Wednesday night, works Tuesday through Friday from 5:00 to 8:00 PM.

Alice — Receptionist in dentist's office, divorced, loves to ski, has six-year-old daughter and four-year-old son.

April — In political science class, wants to be an attorney, loves horses, going to Aruba over winter break.

John really wanted to develop a relationship with April. As they were college classmates, he was able to easily discover a few bits of information about her. When he ran into her during registration for the following semester, he was confident enough to approach her and begin a conversation. The information he had gathered helped him break the ice. Their conversation went like this:

John: Hi, April. How was Aruba?

April: Oh, it was great. My friends and I had a wonderful time. I'm sorry, but I forgot your name.

John: It's John. We were in Dr. Wilson's political science class last semester.

April: Oh, that's right. I remember.

John: You have a great tan.

April: Actually, I *had* a great tan, but it's starting to fade now. My girlfriends and I spent most of our days on the beach. It was so relaxing.

John: Did you happen to go horseback riding on the beach while you were there?

April: No, but I'm sure I would've loved it. I can't believe you remembered that I like horseback riding.

John: April, I remember most things about nice people.

April: Oh, that's so sweet.

John: Do you ride horses in the winter?

April: Not really. It's usually too cold for me.

John: What do you enjoy doing during the winter?

April: I guess I like to go to the movies and out to eat.

John: Me, too. And if that's an invitation, I immediately accept!

April: *(Laughs)* You're funny, John.

John: Feed me and entertain me, and I'm a happy camper.

April: *(Laughs again)* Have you seen any good movies lately?

John: I was so busy with holiday parties and family get-togethers over winter break that I didn't have a chance to see any movies. Are there any good ones out there?

April: Oh, yes. Actually there are a couple of movies that look pretty interesting.

John: Want to join me for dinner and a movie this weekend? It would certainly be the highlight of my semester.

April: I think that would be nice.

John: Great! Let me have your phone number, and I'll call you later so we can make definite plans.

April: Okay, it's 555-5045. If I'm not home, leave a message on my machine. As a matter of fact, let me have your number in case you can't reach me.

In this example, John's list provided him with the right ammunition to press a few of April's hot buttons. Most of the conversation was centered around April's interests, and John was clever enough to pepper their chat with a few compliments and some humor. Also, he was able to connect with her on common ground—dinner and movies. Although John was a little aggressive, his use of humor and sincerity helped him create a subtle urgency with April, in terms of when they'd be speaking again, to make plans for their date.

If you put the same amount of effort and preparation into developing your prospect list as you do other priorities in your life, you'll find that this list of information will yield a gold mine of opportunities for you. These opportunities will lead you to dates and, hopefully, fulfilling relationships.

QUALIFYING YOUR PROSPECTS

It's important for you to be aware of the qualities you desire in another person and to assess each prospect accordingly as time passes. An excellent way for you to develop this framework is to prepare a list of your requirements. If your prospects do well when assessed by this list as you find out more about them, you know you'll be spending quality time with people who interest you. In the sales field, this is called "qualifying the prospect." It helps to determine which prospects have the strongest potential to become a sale.

Know your absolute, non-negotiable requirements for potential prospects. You may be a nonsmoker who doesn't want to be around a smoker. Perhaps you practice a certain religion and don't want to become involved with anyone outside of that religion. These are non-negotiable requirements.

Does it matter to you if a prospect has been married before and has children? Although some people may find this situation okay, others may find it unacceptable. A parent may put his children first, before you. If this does not suit you, then date only people who are single or divorced with no children, and make this one of your non-negotiable requirements.

How about physical characteristics? Does your dream mate have to have dark hair? Light hair? Or does it matter? What about height and weight? Must the prospect have a good physique? Just be careful not to be overly critical when listing your requirements. Try to be realistic in your expectations. Don't allow the slightest flaw or weakness to eliminate a potential prospect.

If you devise a list of requirements, you have a tool with which to assess your prospects. What's the most effective way to get the information necessary to qualify your prospects? First, ask thought-provoking questions that involve more than just a yes or no response. This shows you are genuinely interested in the other person. At the same time, the responses will give you a splendid idea as to whether or not the prospect meets your qualifications. Also, if you are shy, quiet, or a poor conversationalist, asking questions will help take the pressure to speak off your shoulders.

Second, be an attentive listener. A good listener is one who maintains eye contact with the speaker, does not interrupt, and stays focused on the answers. Someone who truly knows how to listen will never make a person feel that he must hurry up to finish a story. An attentive listener makes that person feel as though every word he says is important and interesting.

A WORD TO THE WISE

Qualifying your prospects is important when seeking out someone special, but try not to act like a Gestapo commandant who is interrogating a prisoner. Don't appear to be one step away from demanding a lie detector test and a urine sample! And try not to jump to immediate judgements once you learn something does not fully match up with your list of requirements—if that "something" is a negotiable term. If you are too critical, most of your potential prospects will be disqualified for one reason or another.

You can always find something not to like about another person. But are you being realistic and fair when it comes to eliminating the prospect? Try to seek out the good qualities in a person and do your best to overlook minimal imperfections. That being said, certainly don't settle for someone who is not likely to be a good match for you.

3

Preparing to Meet Someone

There are two main, incredibly simple steps to meeting someone. Well, let's rephrase that. The steps themselves are simple, but knowing how to put them into practice . . . ah, that can be a bit more difficult. (But then again, that's what the rest of this book is about.)

The first step to meeting someone is being in the right place at the right time. Of course, this meeting doesn't necessarily have to happen by chance or coincidentally. Luck and fate certainly play a role, but you must help yourself along. If you see an attractive prospect, it shouldn't matter where you are. You are in the right place and it is the right time! You have the power. Just do things. Get out there. Go where single prospects are likely to be found. Part II will offer some great ideas.

Once you find yourself in the right place at the right time, it is time for step two—doing something constructive in order to connect with that person. When you find yourself in a situation in which an encounter is likely to occur, it's up to you to take the necessary action to make contact with that prospect. Naturally, there are different approaches for different situations. But scores of creative icebreakers are at your disposal. These icebreakers are designed to help you make the initial contact with a person, as well as, hopefully, elicit a positive response. Chapters 4 and 5 include quite a few attention getters and icebreakers to get you started. First, however, an important concept needs to be discussed—increasing your odds for success.

As a single person who is interested in meeting other singles, you should constantly strive to stack all possible odds in your favor. In the previous chapters we have discussed the best ways for you to "package" yourself for the most effective presentation. We have also pointed out valuable listing tactics so that you can accumulate information on prospects and identify what is important. Now that you know how to look your best and you have a good idea of what to look for in a prospect, how can you increase the likelihood of meeting others? Through two general techniques—playing the numbers game and being on twenty-four-hour-a-day alert.

PLAYING THE NUMBERS GAME

Playing the numbers game is a technique that incorporates the concept of networking. When you network, you use everyone you know to introduce you to—or "fix you up" with—other single people.

Playing the numbers game increases your odds of meeting eligible prospects. Basically, you should be ready, willing, and able to seize every opportunity to meet new people. The more people you meet, the better your chances are of finding that special someone.

Sources to tap for networking are family members, friends, neighbors, business associates, and virtually anyone else you know. It is not a disgrace to make it known that you are single and interested in meeting the right person. "If you know someone nice, I would like to meet her," is all you need to say in order to get the ball rolling. If you are genuinely sincere, people will hear you and try to help. Haven't you noticed that almost everyone seems to know someone she would like to introduce to another person?

It is important for you to meet as many prospects as you can. It is equally important to be polite to every person that you meet. Even if a meeting doesn't lead to romance, it might evolve into a good friendship. And who knows, maybe that initial "set-up" will be just the person who introduces you to that special someone later on.

Be sure to thank the person who set up your introduction, even if things don't work out. In addition to being the polite thing to do, it will keep the door open for future introductions through this person.

If you are willing to network, your chances of meeting the right person will greatly increase. You'll have the power of numbers in your favor. There is an old saying among salespeople: "Throw enough garbage against the wall and a certain amount is going to stick." Just as in sales, you may have to meet hundreds of potential prospects before you meet the one person who is truly suitable for you. So play the numbers game.

TWENTY-FOUR-HOUR-A-DAY ALERT

The philosophy of this book is a proactive one: At all times, be physically, mentally, and emotionally prepared to attract and meet a potential love interest. That means always having a pen within your reach to receive or give a telephone number. If a piece of paper, matchbook cover, or cocktail napkin is not available, it means you have to be willing to have a telephone number temporarily written on your hand, arm, knee, or whatever bodily appendage is readily (and appropriately) accessible! This willingness will undoubtedly demonstrate to your prospect an immediate desire and enthusiasm on your part, which will score points for you.

Being on twenty-four-hour-a-day alert means looking attractive, acting upbeat, and being prepared to meet a potential prospect at any time. You have to be prepared when you're walking your dog whether it's 10:30 at night or 6:00 in the morning, running out to the convenience store for a quart of milk, or taking a walk to the corner mailbox. In other words, you should feel confident enough in your appearance to be ready to meet potential prospects anytime and anywhere. If you don't, you'll be doing yourself a great disservice. Don't think it's enough to be armed and ready on Friday and Saturday evenings!

For example, what happens when you see someone who makes your heart pound uncontrollably and gives you goose bumps from your nose to your toes? If you don't feel confident enough in the way you look, you will probably let the opportunity to meet that person slip away. Your dream mate will drive off into the sunset, and you'll want to drive off a cliff out of frustration. Surely you can think of at least one time in your life when you wished you had made contact with someone you were attracted to. Didn't you feel a little disappointed in yourself for letting the opportunity pass you by?

It is not uncommon for people to meet future mates in the most unexpected places, at the most unexpected times. There are lots of stories about couples who would never have guessed they'd find their true loves in a health food market after work, a veterinary clinic during a routine visit, or at the local newspaper stand at lunchtime. You simply do not know when you will come into contact with a wonderful prospect. Isn't it worth a few minutes to prepare yourself just in case?

By the way, if you're a woman, we're not suggesting that you spend an hour putting on make-up before you go out for that quart of milk.

Nor do we recommend that a man spend time shaving before he goes out to walk the dog. Do the best you can, within reason, to make yourself neat and appealing. It's worth the extra few minutes at home grooming yourself before stepping outside. Perhaps you can throw on your favorite pair of jeans instead of those coffee-stained sweatpants. Maybe you can give your hair a quick brush, apply a little lip gloss, use a bit of cologne. The extra effort will give you an extra edge of confidence, which may help you meet the love of your life—the one you won't let get away.

A WORD TO THE WISE

As we've acknowledged before, the singles scene takes courage and energy. But for the most part, friends and acquaintances love to help out. In fact, many enjoy playing matchmaker and bringing two like-minded people together—at least for an evening. So don't be embarrassed to put your name and number out there. A willingness to network shows that you are fun and open-minded. Couple that with being on a relatively constant "state of alert" and you've stacked the odds in your favor. It all comes down to seizing any opportunity that comes your way.

4

Breaking the Ice With Attention Getters

*D*o you feel confident about starting a conversation with an interesting prospect? If so, you can turn to Chapter 5 right now and start choosing some icebreaking lines. But, like many people, you may cringe at the thought of having to use a line to meet an attractive prospect. Why? It could be due to a fear of rejection or finding yourself at a loss for words. It could also stem from a concern that you'll come off sounding desperate, aggressive, corny, hokey, or insincere.

Here's the good news! There are ways to initiate an encounter with a person without having to say a word. For example, carrying an interesting book or wearing a funny T-shirt can compel a person to speak to you. It's a great way to shift the burden of starting a conversation into the hands of interesting prospects.

The following icebreaking attention getters are designed to attract prospects and get them to start a conversation with you. You won't have to say a word to generate the initial contact. Prospects will be encouraged to approach you, wherever you may be. Although there are many creative things you can do to achieve this attention, we have focused on some of the more interesting examples.

MAGAZINES, BOOKS, AND BROCHURES

Carry a book or magazine with a fascinating title. The more interesting the title, the more likely it is to produce a comment or query from a prospect. Be sure to carry or read the book in a way that leaves the front cover exposed, and be sure to take it everywhere you go.

Women may choose to carry books and magazines that are likely to appeal to men. Examples of such magazines include *Sports Illustrated*,

Baseball Digest, Car and Driver, and *Popular Mechanics.* Good book choices might include *Jordan Rules, Sting Like a Bee, Wealth Without Risk,* and *How I Made a Million Dollars in Mail Order.*

Men might choose to read or carry magazines that would pique a woman's interest enough to cause her to make a comment. Magazines such as *Gourmet, Travel & Leisure,* and *New Yorker* are good choices. Book selections might include *The History of God, Success Forces, Life's Little Instruction Book,* and *Aliens Among Us.* These, and plenty of other books or magazines, are likely to evoke comments and spark conversations.

Are you a science buff—or at least want to be one? Take a *Scientific American* with you. There is always an intriguing cover, and you will appear quite intellectual! If you are into fitness and want to meet people of similar interests, try carrying *Life Extension* or *Yoga Journal* magazine. It will be evident that you care about your body and your mind. That's attractive! And such magazines are not so specialized or advanced that the average person couldn't read and relate to them. A good prospect might very well say, "I've been meaning to learn more about that."

By the way, if you happen to see a possible prospect reading an interesting book or magazine, don't let the opportunity pass you by; break the ice with a comment of your own. Express your interest in the book or magazine and, rest assured, a conversation will follow. Carry on from there!

Also consider carrying travel literature with you. Travel brochures are easy to bring with you to work, meeting places, restaurants, and other public places. They are great conversation starters. Lay them out or carry them in plain view. While you leaf through the brochures, don't be surprised if people who happen to be nearby begin to comment. They may ask you questions, offer suggestions ("I hear there's a fabulous seafood restaurant there called . . ."), or share a personal experience or two that they had while vacationing in the same location.

PETS

Many congenial people cannot resist a friendly dog. So take your dog for leisurely walks through your neighborhood (or any neighborhood for that matter). You never know whom you'll run into. If you take the dog to a park or beach, bring a toy for it to play with. Be sure to throw the ball or toy near any attractive prospects you see in order to get closer and attract his attention.

Although any type of dog can be a good conversation starter, unique breeds are even better. Another good idea is to fasten a big bow or brightly colored bandanna around the dog's neck—then you're in business. If you don't have a dog, you could always borrow one from a relative, neighbor, or friend.

This technique for starting a conversation can also work with other pets, such as cats and birds, although you'll have to be careful of what you do and where you go. It's certainly not a good idea to take your bird for a walk in the park! A cat, on the other hand, might feel perfectly comfortable on a leash if you are walking in a relatively quiet area. Never underestimate what a furry friend can do for your social life!

KIDS

Think of how most adults might react to seeing a little girl pushing her doll carriage in the park or a small boy playing one of his first baseball games. "She's like a doll! How old is she?" "I remember when my dad taught me how to hit a ball!" Kids provide great material for conversations.

On the weekend, take your child/children/nephew/niece/neighbor's child out to the park, playground, or beach for an afternoon of fun. Bring some sports equipment, toys, snacks, blankets, and books. Set yourself up in a visible, grassy place, if possible. Don't be surprised at how often you are approached by divorced or single parents. You might find yourself easily gliding into a conversation on the latest trends in toys and the best pop-up books.

Keep in mind, men and women with kids always seem easy to approach. Most likely, a prospect will assume you are a concerned and giving person because you have chosen to spend a free afternoon with a little one—unless, of course, you are screaming at the child and hoarding all of the pretzels!

CAMCORDERS AND CAMERAS

Go to a park or beach with your camcorder or camera. They're great conversation starters. When a prospect breaks the ice and asks what you're filming or taking pictures of, be ready with an interesting response that will initiate a conversation. If you're somewhat aggressive, you could respond to the question with something like, "I'm creating an album on the beauty of nature, and I think you're a natural beauty. I'd love to include a picture of you in my album." Or you could be subtler and talk about how much you appreciate a rustic or natural landscape. Then ask if your prospect is familiar with other local areas that would be worth filming.

If you have your pet with you, approach a prospect and ask if he would please take a picture of you with your pet. In appreciation of the favor, offer to treat the person to ice cream or even lunch! Even better, offer to take a picture of your prospect and promise to e-mail a copy to him. When you send the photo, be sure to include a short, warm note.

SPORTS EQUIPMENT

Plan a sports outing with some of your friends. Tennis, volleyball, baseball, basketball, Frisbee, and biking are good choices. The sheer fact that you are armed with fun equipment and hyped up for an afternoon outdoors will be attractive to like-minded prospects. If someone interesting does approach you, invite him to join your team for a game. Even if he declines, perhaps due to shyness or time constraints, your friendly and easy-going attitude will open the door for further conversation.

Here's another great idea. Before and/or after the outing, plan to stop somewhere for a meal or snack. Be sure to carry your equipment into the snack bar or restaurant and place it near you—on the table or counter, if it fits. The sight of the equipment will more than likely elicit responses from other customers.

KITES

Perfect to fly at a beach or park, kites are great attention getters and conversation starters. Kites have been around for quite a while, but the beauty of a colorful and high-flying kite never goes out of style. Many people just love to watch a kite ride the wind. You very well might ignite nostalgia in and see a broad smile on the face of a passerby. If that person seems like an interesting prospect, ask if he is an expert kite-flyer or offer to let him try his hand at it.

Don't get upset if you can't seem to keep your kite airborne; an attractive prospect may offer to help. And don't forget, you can always use this opportunity to seek help from a passerby—the right passerby, of course.

FUN HAIRSTYLES

There are certainly many things you can carry, and many creatures you can bring along, in order to catch the eye of a possible prospect. However, you don't need extras—you, yourself, are a fantastic conversation piece! There's lots of style changes you can do to turn heads. One of the quickest and easiest methods is to try a new hairstyle.

Muster up some courage! In order to generate attention, try something different or even outrageous. Men, if your hair is normally short, try growing a ponytail. If you are used to wearing long hair, get a crew cut or shave your head. Facial hair is another possible avenue for change. Grow or remove beards and mustaches. Sexy goatees and stylized sideburns get noticed.

Women, dye or rinse your hair with a bold new color. Grow it long, cut it short, braid it, curl it, or adorn it with pretty accessories. Whether a sleek up-sweep or a buoyant bob, try something new to draw interest and comments from possible prospects. The change will give you confidence, as well.

UNIQUE CLOTHING AND ACCESSORIES

Looking for attention? The details on your clothing and the accessories you select can grab attention and break the ice faster than a planned conversation. Let's start with some easy-to-find clothing items and move on from there.

T-shirts are All-American pieces of clothing that no one would want to live without. We love to throw on a comfy T-shirt when watching a good movie or doing late-night work. But did you ever think a T-shirt could be the catalyst for a relationship? Well, it can. Wear a brightly colored T-shirt with an interesting slogan or artwork and you are sure to get noticed! Things like the name of your favorite band, vacation spots, and television shows are good choices to display on T-shirts, as well. Interesting sayings and even pictures will also attract attention.

There are hats, too, for those of us who like to be "*ahead* of the game"! Wear a snazzy, fashionable, or outrageous hat and you're apt to get lots of comments. If you have a face for hats and a flair for the creative, give this idea a fling.

If you jog, work out, dance, or are involved in any sports activity, wear a brightly colored headband or baseball cap to get attention. If the band bears the name of your favorite sports team, that's even better. You may get comments from prospects who either love or hate your team. Either response is fine as long as it promotes some interaction.

The smaller items count too. Put on a pair of unique, wildly colored socks, or a vibrant, flashy tie. Not only are such clothing items fun additions to your wardrobe, they are sure-fire attention getters too!

You may or may not be a "foot person," but plenty of people are drawn to trendy shoes. Why not explore your foot fashion sense? Women have countless options, from sexy stilettos to stylish sling-backs. Even funky flip-flops are a craze these days, with jeweled straps and colorful soles! And men's foot fashions keep expanding as well. For example, polished dress loafers let a woman know you are youthful yet have class. Well-cut, thick-soled tie shoes show you are well-grounded *and* up-to-date. Some people say it's all in the details!

Definitely consider wearing an interesting piece of jewelry. It is one of the best ways to start a conversation. Both men and women can use this attention-getting tactic with ease. Ethnic designs, uncommon stones, hand-carved crafts, and heirloom pieces are beautiful ways to get noticed. Just be sure to wear something that *you* like—something that matches your personality well.

Lastly, you could always sport a button that makes a statement, asks a question, or touts your personal cause. Most people don't wear buttons on their clothing anymore, but putting them on backpacks, tote bags, and pocketbooks is completely acceptable. Sit back and be prepared for some responses. Your button might say, "Single and Miserable," "Party Animal," "My Lawyer Can Beat Up Your Lawyer," "Lose Weight Now... Ask Me How," "Ask Me What Planet I'm On," "Help the Homeless," "Stop Animal Testing," and so on. Make sure the button is large enough to read and interesting enough to provoke a response.

A WORD TO THE WISE

These are just a few of the many ways to effectively get yourself noticed. Try out the ones that you feel most comfortable with. And remember, these attention-getting strategies are limited only by your sense of adventure and imagination.

There's just one note of caution: Be creative, not eccentric. While it is good to be bold and appear different, avoid going out of your way to be weird. You might scare off good prospects if you go too far with the attention getters. So have fun, but don't get to a point where the attention is negative. If you are too flamboyant or corny, you might make others feel uncomfortable.

5

Starting a Conversation

*S*ome people are able to talk easily and naturally in any situation. Others seem to get tongue-tied whenever they open their mouths (except when they're eating!). Unless you have eyes that speak for you, you're going to need conversation skills in order to break the ice during your first encounter with a prospect. It's one thing to grab someone's attention with an eye-catching accessory or a witty comment. But initiating a conversation is a whole different matter.

Let's say that you feel a strong attraction to someone. Along with this attraction, you may also experience some nervousness or anxiety in initiating verbal contact. You may feel intense pressure to say the right thing. The fear of rejection may also be on your mind, complicating your dilemma even further. Additionally, your brain may remind you that the person you want to approach is a complete stranger— what is this person going to think of you? How is she going to respond to your approach? All of these insecurities can cause you to feel uncomfortable about initiating that first contact.

So, how do you get things started? How can you rid yourself of these anxieties and feel confident enough to break the ice? Read on.

HAVING A HEALTHY ATTITUDE

Before you approach your prospect, get yourself into a positive state of mind. Remind yourself that what you are about to do is normal, constructive, and friendly. By conversing with a prospect, you simply make known that you are social and interested in others. There is nothing wrong or desperate about that! Communicate a light, carefree, "what-the-heck" attitude for the initial contact.

Keep in mind that your first contact with another person doesn't necessarily have to be a verbal one. Be creative in your approach. Do whatever it takes, within reason, to get that person to notice you. For example, in bars and dance clubs it is acceptable to have a bartender or waitress deliver a drink with your compliments to someone you're admiring. This tactic is sure to get you noticed, and you never know what might develop after that. We know of a certain gentleman who employs a creative variation on this approach. When he is out having breakfast, he has the waitress bring a glass of freshly squeezed orange juice along with a short pleasant note to someone he finds attractive. He continually meets and dates attractive women this way.

However, the conversation must begin at some point. Start with an icebreaker, and if it leads to conversation, act interested and sincere—don't be intense or offensive.

CHOOSING A GOOD ICEBREAKER

Let's assume that you're ready. You've packaged yourself in the best possible way, you're in the right place at the right time, and you see someone who interests you. So what do you do now? Well, you can't wait for your prospect to make the first move (although it sure would be nice, wouldn't it?). You've got to begin the conversation yourself.

This is probably one of the hardest phases of meeting someone, especially if you are shy. Generally, it's much easier to answer someone else's question than it is to pose one of your own. But what if your prospect doesn't make the first move? Are you willing to let that person slip away? What can you say (with a minimal amount of trembling) to start things off?

The initial verbal contact should begin with a one-liner to break the ice—either a question or statement. Your question might be funny, designed to get the person to giggle, or it might be more serious, intended to elicit a thought-out response. Your statement might be an opinion that you expect the person to agree or even disagree with, or a comment that you hope will be met with an interested reply. Need a little help? This chapter includes lots of icebreakers to get you started, and Part II has many more.

You will notice that the icebreaking lines are preceded by checkboxes. Whenever you come across an icebreaker that fits your personality, check its box. Later, when reviewing this book for ideas and support, you'll be able to find your favorites quickly and easily. Feel free to use these lines exactly as they are written, modify them to fit your personal style, or use them as a springboard to create lines of your own. The options are limitless.

Start out by selecting a few icebreakers, and practice saying them out loud while standing in front of a mirror. Get used to the way they sound. Try delivering the lines to a family member or friend and gauge the reaction. After all, if a line is stupid, do you really want to use it? On the other hand, if your "audience" likes what you're saying and the confident manner of your delivery, you'll probably feel more comfortable trying that line on a prospect. Practicing will help you rid yourself of anxiety. In a while, your line delivery will be so natural that your icebreakers won't be confused with come-ons. When it's time for the actual line delivery, you'll sound smooth, confident, and natural. Rehearsing is the key.

You can even keep a list of your favorite icebreakers in a handy place, such as your wallet or pocketbook. If you feel it is necessary, quickly review the list right before you approach your prospect. Then go for it!

Tried-and-True Icebreaking Lines

The following list includes some of the simplest things to say to another person in order to initiate contact and generate conversation. Realize that these lines by themselves won't establish a long-term relationship, but they can get another person to notice you and respond to what you have said.

Different lines are better suited for different personalities. No one will feel truly comfortable with all of the lines found in this book. Select only those that you feel most at ease with. Keep in mind that the success of these lines largely depends on your delivery. Creative lines may require effective voice inflections, facial expressions, or body mannerisms—all of which you will develop through experience. Just remember, above all, use only those lines that feel right to you and that most closely reflect your personality.

Approach your prospect, establish eye contact, and confidently say:

❑ "Hi, my name is _____. What's yours?"

❑ "Hi, what's your name? Mine's _____."

❑ "Excuse me, do I know you from somewhere?" *(This is one of the old-*

est yet most effective lines used. However, you must sound sincere or the line will come off as a come-on!)

❏ "Do you come here often?"

❏ "What do you think of this place?"

❏ "What have you heard about this place?"

❏ "Some weather, isn't it?"

❏ "This place is really nice, isn't it?"

❏ "Have you ever been here before?"

❏ "Do you live around here?"

❏ "Gee, I'm sorry. Did I bump into you?"

❏ "Can I help you with that?"

❏ "Here, let me get that for you."

❏ "Excuse me, do you have the time?"

❏ "Have I met you before? You look so familiar."

❏ "May I ask you a question?" *(Make sure you have a good question or two to ask when the prospect says yes.)*

❏ "Do you mind my telling you how good you look in that _____?" *(Insert appropriate article of clothing.)*

❏ "Will you forgive me for saying that you look great in that color? It really brings out the beauty of your eyes/skin/hair."

❏ "Do you mind my telling you that you remind me of (my) _____?" *(Insert the name of a friend, relative, or celebrity.)*

❏ "You look like someone I know I would want to meet."

❏ "I wish I had the perfect line to get you to start talking to me, but I don't. So how about if I just say, 'Hi, my name is _____'?"

More Icebreaking Lines

The icebreaking lines presented above are very basic. Sometimes, however, you may be in a more humorous or playful mood, or the situation may call for a more imaginative icebreaker. Many of the following lines may sound slightly unusual, but one may be just perfect for that non-basic moment.

An unusual icebreaker can be more fun. And no matter what you say, remember that the icebreaker's goal is to open the door to conversation. Because of this, even a negative response from your prospect is better than no response at all. You can always follow up on the negative reaction with a comment such as, "Well, I guess that was a pretty stupid thing to say, but I wasn't sure of the best way to come over and say hello. Do you forgive me?" or "Okay, I'll admit that that was a corny line, but I really just wanted to talk to you." Such follow-up lines often smooth ruffled feathers and neutralize initial negative reactions.

As with the tried-and-true icebreakers, some of the following lines will roll off your tongue, while others will catch in your throat. Read through the lines and check those that best fit your personal style. Practice saying the lines to yourself in the mirror, to your dog, and to attractive characters on the television screen. When ready to use a line, approach your prospect and establish eye contact first.

❑ "I hope the rest of my day looks as good as you do."

❑ "Excuse me, but how does someone become a member of your fan club?"

❑ "The moment I saw you, I knew I wanted to be your friend."

❑ "You look incredible. May I have a picture of you to put on my refrigerator door?"

❑ "You're the type of person I've always dreamed about."

❑ "I would follow you anywhere."

❑ "I feel thoroughly enriched after seeing you."

❑ "You look like a million bucks after taxes."

❑ "I'd love to hold hands with you. My fingers would be ecstatic."

❑ "I think I'm falling in like with you."

❑ "You have pretty eyes. Are they real?" *(To be said with obvious humor.)*

❑ "Do you have a quarter? My mom told me to call her when I found the girl/guy of my dreams."

❑ "Do you know anyone who is exactly like you in every way but isn't currently involved with someone?"

❑ "If I had to, I'd get a second job just to be with you on a first date."

❑ "I'm touched by this chance encounter with you. Would you care to honor this special occasion and join me for some cookies and milk?"

❑ "I have to get to know you."

❑ "You look good enough to be on a picture postcard."

❑ "On a scale of one to ten, you break the scales in a good way."

❑ "One look at you and it's impossible to ignore you."

❑ "I can't let you walk by without at least opening the door for you."

❑ "I don't think I could ever get tired of looking at you."

❑ "You're definitely worth a second glance."

❑ "When you meet someone new, you can be either honest or phony. All I can do with you is speak from my heart."

❑ "I just bought this book and I'd like to try one of the icebreaking lines in order to meet you. I really want it to work, so would you tell me what you think?" *(Use this line anywhere and on anyone. Simply show the book to your prospect, then watch that person immediately smile or break into a good-natured laugh. This line works like a charm because it disarms the prospect, letting her know you are sincere in your effort to meet her. This may be one of the best icebreaking lines of all.)*

Any of the icebreaking lines (or modifications of these lines) can be starters in your attempt to meet people. And be aware that they are exactly that—starters. Please realize that it *usually* takes more than an icebreaker to get a conversation flowing. Always arm yourself with a few follow-up lines that you can use in response to a prospect's reaction to your initial icebreaker. Keep some appropriate comments, questions, or other icebreakers up your sleeve. Remember, even a creative icebreaker can meet with a dead-end reaction, and you must always be ready to meet such reactions head-on.

To further illustrate this point, let's say you are at a dance club and see someone you'd like to meet. You walk over and initiate contact with this person by using an icebreaker:

> *You:*   Excuse me, do you have the time?
>
> *Prospect:*   9:30.

Okay, now what? You've broken the ice and made initial contact, but what next? You must be ready with another line:

> *You:*   Do you think you could give me the next five minutes?
>
> *Prospect:* Well, uh, I guess so.

You seem to have hit a dead end. Looks like you have to work a little harder:

> *You:*   Is this the first time you've been here? I don't remember seeing you here before.
>
> *Prospect:* Yes, it is. A couple of my friends came here last week and they really loved it. I can see why. The decor is great and . . .

Well, congratulations! It took a little more than a simple icebreaker to get a dialogue going, but you hung in there and did it.

Let's take a look at another hypothetical situation in which the importance of having follow-up phrases is illustrated. You find yourself in the same dance club:

> *You:*   This place is really nice, isn't it?
>
> *Prospect:* Yes, it is.

Here's that old familiar dead end, but you're going to face it head on with a little humor:

> *You:*   So, do you think this is the spot where they found the body? *(Pause)* Just kidding.
>
> *Prospect:* *(Laughs)* Cute.

Once again, being armed with follow-up material helped you pave the way for a conversation.

You want one more dance-club scenario? Okay then, here goes:

> *You:*   Excuse me, but how does one become a member of your fan club?
>
> *Prospect:* *(Mildly annoyed)* Excuse me?

> *You:*   I just wanted to know how to join your fan club.
>
> *Prospect:*   *(More annoyed)* You can't.

Now there's a dead end if ever there was one. You may simply decide to lick your wounded ego and walk away before more damage is done. On the other hand, if you're adventurous, you might choose to give it one more shot:

> *You:*   Look, I know that was a really corny line. I guess I just didn't know how to meet you. All I wanted to do was say hello.
>
> *Prospect:*   Well, at least that's a little more direct. I don't think I've seen you here before . . .

Okay, so we've given this last scene somewhat of a happy ending. Of course, the prospect just as easily could have turned her back on your final attempt. And that is certainly something you should be prepared for. Just remember not to take a negative reaction too personally. You can't expect each and every person to be receptive to your attempts at conversation. Learn from these experiences.

Once again, the important thing is to be prepared with more than just the simple icebreaker when you approach someone. Always have a few good follow-ups to help get that conversation off the ground. More on possible responses to your icebreakers and how to effectively follow them up is presented in Chapter 6. And don't forget to check Part II for many more unusual, creative icebreakers.

A WORD TO THE WISE

Know that many individuals who have become skilled at meeting other people have not always been so successful. More than likely, they have experienced failure in at least some of their attempts. However, let's not use the word "failure." Rather, let's say that they haven't always succeeded. Practice, diligence, and the ability to bounce back helped them sharpen their confrontational skills.

You (like everyone else) will experience setbacks from time to time. Don't be discouraged by "non-successes." No matter how many times you don't succeed, always remember that it takes only one victory to land your true love.

6

Following Up and Closing the Deal

Okay, you've broken the ice. The prospect who has made your heart flutter at first sight has noticed you. Maybe your clever icebreaker made that person laugh, smile, or respond positively. Or your attention-getting conversation starter caused him to take the first step in verbally breaking the ice with you. For whatever reason, you now have your prospect's undivided attention. Where do you go from here? To the follow-up, of course.

In order for you to quickly develop stimulating conversation, try working initially within the context of the icebreaker. If this line directly focused on your prospect, stretch that icebreaker to include more conversation about him. Minimize focus on yourself and keep the spotlight on the other person. Not only will this prevent you from seeming self-centered, the attention will flatter your prospect. However, if your prospect directs the conversation to you, then by all means feel free to talk about yourself. Just don't get carried away. After a reasonable amount of time, return the focus to your prospect.

In order to continue a conversation, you must be able to follow up your prospect's response. Naturally, your follow-up depends on the kind of response you get. In this chapter, we anticipate several possible responses and give you pointers on how to further converse.

TYPES OF RESPONSES AND FOLLOW-UPS

People are unique, and their reactions to you can be equally unique. Your attempts at conversation can be met with responses that range from extremely positive to intensely negative. It's important for you to know when to respond and when not to, when to continue your efforts and when to head for the hills. You should be able to masterfully handle virtually any type of response you get, whether it's a direct answer to a question, a sly innuendo, a snide comment, another question, a heated objection, or complete disinterest. Let's discuss some of the more common responses and include suggestions on how you might effectively follow them up.

Nonverbal Responses

What do you do if someone smiles, nods his head, or laughs at your opening question or line, but doesn't say anything? If you're nervous, your initial reaction may be to run. Don't. Give it another shot. Even a very simple question or statement can be useful:

❏ "What's your name?"

❏ "Do you like it here?"

❏ "It's pretty noisy in here; let me repeat my question."

Such follow-ups might be just enough to pave the way for additional exchange. Once your prospect has responded with something (anything!), move on to more open-ended types of questions and try to get a more meaningful conversation going.

If all your attempts are unsuccessful, then it's probably a good idea to move on. Don't view this as a rejection, and don't take it personally. In all likelihood, there are any number of reasons that the person may not have responded positively to you.

Brief Verbal Responses

If your prospect responds to you verbally, although briefly, at least you've got something to go on. Follow up specifically on the response. Either make a comment about the situation you're in, or ask a question designed to build upon the prospect's brief response:

❏ "Yes, this really is a nice place."

❏ "What do you mean by . . .?"

❏ "Do you mean that . . .?"

How do you know if the prospect's response is positive? Clues from his facial expression (a smile is better than a frown) and other body language signals (a back turned toward you is not a good sign) are good indicators. If the prospect continues to make eye contact with you, as if awaiting further conversation, it's probably safe to assume the response is positive.

Lengthy Verbal Responses

A more complete verbal response is certainly more encouraging than a brief one. After all, if the prospect isn't interested, he won't say anything to encourage further conversation. Lengthy verbal responses open the door for additional relevant questions and insightful comments. As the conversation continues, don't forget to maintain eye contact and show interest in what your prospect is saying:

❑ "I agree with you . . ."

❑ "That's an interesting point . . ."

❑ "What do you think about . . .?"

The important thing is to keep the communication lines open and the conversation flowing.

Negative Verbal Responses

If your prospect responds verbally in a negative way, you'll have to make the decision to either give it another shot or simply walk away. In all probability, your decision will be based on the type of negative response you receive. If you sense hostility, sarcasm, or a complete "closed door," you may choose to preserve your dignity, say something like, "Nice talking to you," and walk away.

If, on the other hand, the response is verbally negative but the person still seems nice enough, you may want to give it one more try. Here, though, is where you should change directions. If you used humor in your opening line, try to be a little more sensitive and serious now:

❑ "Please forgive my comment/question. I just wanted to say hello, and I thought that my remark might have been the way to do it."

If you were serious—maybe too serious—initially, try to lighten things up a little:

❑ "May I have a glass of water to wash down my foot?"

If this effort doesn't seem to open the door even a little, you may decide to simply cut your losses and move on.

Avoidance Responses

If your prospect totally avoids responding to you, there must be a reason. Maybe the person doesn't speak your language! Maybe he isn't interested in meeting anyone. Of course, there's always the possibility that the person is simply not interested in you. By now, though, you should be psychologically prepared to deal with that possibility.

Should you continue your attempt with this prospect? Probably not—unless you're in a noisy place and there's a possibility that your prospect didn't hear your line. However, if you feel a strong inclination, you could give it one last-ditch effort:

❏ "I'm really having a hard time. I like meeting and getting to know people, but it seems like people aren't responding. Would you please help me? Would you tell me what I'm doing wrong?"

And if this final attempt doesn't work, at least you'll know that you tried. Don't get down on yourself. Give yourself credit for your determination and consider the experience a building block in the foundation of your self-esteem. There are plenty of other people out there for you to meet.

WAYS TO KEEP THE CONVERSATION GOING

If you are like most people, you are probably worried about running out of things to say during a conversation. You may feel pressure to keep the dialogue going because you think you'll be judged on your ability to keep talking. If the conversation stops, you might feel that it's your fault and that your prospect will lose interest in you.

First of all, don't think that you're alone. Most people experience the same concern. It's important for you to realize that conversations are two-way streets. Your prospect has just as much responsibility as you do to keep the dialogue moving along.

However, instead of getting caught up in deciding who's responsible for the death of a conversation, let's discuss what you can do to keep it alive. Back in Chapter 5, we suggested that you jot down a few icebreakers and keep them in your wallet or pocketbook for handy reference. Well, you can use this same technique to keep a conversation flowing. On a separate card or paper, list a number of topics or subjects that you might introduce into a conversation.

Of course, we don't expect you to pull out the card in front of the other person and start reading. Be discreet; rely on the card only if necessary. Excuse yourself and go into the bathroom, where you can glance at the card. If you are stuck, reminding yourself of additional topics will help you inject fresh energy into your exchange.

Below are additional conversational skills to keep in mind when trying to maintain a conversation. They will help stack the odds in your favor for a successful verbal exchange.

- Always get your prospect's name and always give yours. During the course of your conversation, be sure to casually use the other person's name.

- Always try to "connect" with your prospect on any subject or feeling by using appropriate facial expressions and voice inflections. This common bond could cause a prospect to want to see you again.

- Try to identify your prospect's "hot buttons," then zero in on them.

TECHNIQUES TO CLOSE THE DEAL

Let's say that you have gotten some communication going. At this point, you'll need to determine immediately how much time you have for conversation. Most likely, you'll have to "close the deal" or "close the sale" within a brief period of time. In sales, that means making the sale and creating a satisfied customer. Closing the deal in the context of this book means generating enough interest from your prospect to either make plans for a future meeting or, at the very least, exchange phone numbers.

It's critical to get a feeling for how much time you have to close the deal. This time frame will help you decide on the particular closing technique you should use. It's up to you to get the right "feel" for the time factor involved. Your efforts to close the deal will fall short if you don't judge correctly. You don't want your dream prospect darting off and out of your life while you're still in the midst of making conversation!

Once you have determined how much time you have, you'll need to decide which of the three closing techniques you should use to wrap up the deal. Think of your choices as the Quick-Close Technique, the Extended-Close Technique, and the Semi-Date Close Technique. Let's discuss these methods further and see how to apply each one.

Quick-Close Technique

The Quick-Close is described accurately by its name. If either you or your prospect are in a hurry—rushing to catch a train or trying to get to work, school, or a meeting on time—then the Quick-Close is the best technique. If you're in your car and pull up alongside an attractive prospect at a light, you won't have much time to close the deal, will you? This is another instance in which the Quick-Close should be used.

What's the best way to close the deal quickly? Be honest and direct. "I'd love to speak with you more, but it looks like you're in a hurry," or, "I'm in a rush to get to work/catch a train/get to class on time, but I'd really love to speak with you again." These lines must be followed by an attempt to make further contact: "Why don't you give me your phone number and let me know the best time to reach you." Then you should say something like, "I really enjoyed meeting you and look forward to speaking with you soon."

The following conversation, which takes place in a supermarket, illustrates the Quick-Close Technique:

Dave: How does a guy become a member of your fan club?

Kelli: I don't have a fan club.

Dave: You have one now. What's your name?

Kelli: Kelli.

Dave: I'm Dave. It's nice to meet you, Kelli.

Kelli: Thanks. It's nice to meet you, too.

Dave: I shop here regularly. How come I haven't seen you before?

Kelli: I normally don't shop here. My sister and brother live out this way. Tonight, we're having a twenty-fifth-anniversary dinner party for my parents, and I needed to pick up a few things. My sister is waiting for me so we can start cooking.

Dave: What a nice thing to do. Listen, I don't want to keep you. You're obviously in a hurry.

Kelli: Yes, I really am.

Dave: Kelli, I really enjoyed meeting you. And I'd love to speak with you again, and also find out how the dinner went. Can I call you?

Kelli: Well, this is all kind of quick, but why not? My number is 555-2421.

Dave: I hope your parents have a wonderful anniversary, and I'll look forward to speaking with you soon.

Kelli: Likewise.

In this example, Dave used an icebreaker in his initial encounter with Kelli. He quickly determined that she was in a hurry to get her parents' anniversary dinner started, so he chose to use the Quick-Close. Besides Dave's highly complimentary opening icebreaker, he also praised Kelli and her siblings on their thoughtfulness in preparing a special dinner for their parents. Possibly the most important thing Dave did was let Kelli know that he wanted to talk to her again and find out how the dinner went. When using the Quick-Close Technique, it's critical that phone numbers are exchanged or a date is made to insure future contact.

Also important in Dave's initial encounter with Kelli was his wish for the dinner to be successful. This further helped Dave to connect with Kelli, since he showed interest in something that was meaningful to her. When Dave makes his follow-up call to Kelli, his conversation should touch upon her parents' reaction to the dinner, how many people were there, where it was held, if videos or pictures were taken, and so on. Dinner together and the opportunity to see pictures or a video of that anniversary evening would be the perfect follow-up date.

Extended-Close Technique

The Extended-Close is ideally suited for situations in which you've determined that neither you nor your prospect are in a hurry. If you see that you can have ten or fifteen minutes (at least) of pleasant, pressure-free conversation, use the Extended-Close Technique. You'll have more than enough time to establish rapport, generate interest, develop a little chemistry, and either give or receive a phone number.

Let's go back to the grocery store and see how Dave uses the Extended-Close Technique in his first encounter with Kelli:

Dave: How does a guy become a member of your fan club?

Kelli: I don't have a fan club.

Dave: You have one now. What's your name?

Kelli: Kelli.

Dave: I'm Dave. It's nice to meet you, Kelli.

Kelli: Thanks. It's nice to meet you, too.

Dave: I shop here regularly. How come I haven't seen you before?

Kelli: Because I hate grocery shopping and do it only when absolutely necessary.

Dave: Is that the case today?

Kelli: Absolutely!

Dave: Well, Kelli, I'm glad you found it necessary to shop today. You've made it a very special shopping experience for me.

Kelli: (*Laughs*) Don't tell me that you actually like grocery shopping. Or do you?

Dave: I really don't mind it. I like to keep my refrigerator and cupboards stocked. I prefer to cook for myself rather than eat alone in a restaurant.

Kelli: What kind of foods do you like?

Dave: Mostly chicken, some fish, and just about all fresh vegetables. How about you?

Kelli: Pretty much the same, but I would have to add pizza and Thai food to the list.

Dave: I guess I forgot to mention pizza, but I've never had Thai food.

Kelli: Oh, Thai food is wonderful. It offers some very unique taste sensations.

> *Dave:* Sounds interesting. I might like to try it. Is there a particular restaurant you go to for Thai food?
>
> *Kelli:* As a matter of fact, there's a wonderful Thai restaurant that recently opened downtown.
>
> *Dave:* Would you like to go there with me for dinner sometime?
>
> *Kelli:* That invitation is hard to refuse.
>
> *Dave:* Well, let me have your phone number and I'll call you later to firm up some dinner plans.
>
> *Kelli:* All right. It's 555-2421.
>
> *Dave:* When is the best time to call you?
>
> *Kelli:* Most evenings between 8:00 and 10:00.
>
> *Dave:* Great! Listen, Kelli, I really enjoyed meeting you and look forward to having dinner with you soon. I'll call you within the next couple of days.
>
> *Kelli:* That's fine. I'll look forward to hearing from you.

This example shows how Dave, after breaking the ice with Kelli, was able to readily determine that this situation did not require the Quick-Close. At the end of Dave's compliment— ". . .you've made this a very special shopping experience for me"—Kelli laughed and then asked him a question. It was at this point that Dave figured he had enough time to employ the Extended-Close in his encounter with Kelli.

During the course of their conversation, Dave and Kelli "connected" on the topic of foods they liked. Furthermore, Dave zeroed in on Kelli's passion for Thai food and turned it into an offer for a dinner date, which Kelli accepted.

Semi-Date Close Technique

The closing technique that exemplifies the best case scenario is the Semi-Date Close Technique. This occurs when you meet an attractive prospect with whom you immediately seem to hit it off. Neither of you is under pressure to leave, and, because you are enjoying each other's company, you decide to go somewhere else together.

Let's say you meet someone while browsing in a bookstore, and then the two of you decide to go for a walk in the park. During your walk, you agree to stop for lunch at a local café. You have converted a casual meeting with your prospect into a semi-date. Of course, this may not be an "official" (prearranged) date, but such an impromptu experience has great odds of evolving into future official dates.

Let's see how our friend Dave uses the Semi-Date Close in his first encounter with Kelli:

Dave: How does a guy become a member of your fan club?

Kelli: I don't have a fan club.

Dave: You have one now. What's your name?

Kelli: Kelli.

Dave: I'm Dave. It's nice to meet you, Kelli.

Kelli: Thanks. It's nice to meet you, too.

Dave: I shop here regularly. How come I haven't seen you before?

Kelli: I don't know. I guess it's just been bad timing for you.

Dave: *(Laughs)* Yes, I suppose I should thank fate.

Kelli: Actually, you should probably thank my boss. I've got a certain amount of sick days from work, and I'm taking one today.

Dave: Are you sick?

Kelli: No, I'm just taking the day and glad that I'm not working.

Dave: I'm also glad you're not working.

Kelli: Well, thanks.

Dave: So what else have you got planned for the day?

Kelli: Well, I'm just picking up a few bare essentials here, then I figured I'd stop at the flea market around the corner and check out the bargains.

Dave: I love bargains. Would you mind if I joined you, Kelli?

Kelli:	That would be nice. But don't you have to go to work today?
Dave:	No. Today's my day off and I have nothing planned. As a matter of fact, I'd like to treat you to lunch after the flea market.
Kelli:	Sounds okay to me.
Dave:	Let's put the grocery bags in our cars, then we can walk to the flea market.
Kelli:	Great idea, Dave. It's a beautiful day and I'd love the exercise.

Early in their conversation, Dave discovered that Kelli had the day off from work, so he quickly assessed that there was no pressure for the Quick-Close. When Kelli teased Dave about his "bad timing" at never having run into her before, Dave felt that Kelli was mildly flirting with him, so he was comfortable in continuing the conversation. It didn't take long for him to sense a mutual attraction, a rapport, so he decided to attempt the Semi-Date Close, which yielded positive results.

A WORD TO THE WISE

With today's fast-paced lifestyles, people are on the go much more than they might like to be. It is for this single reason that you should always be prepared to use the Quick-Close Technique in your encounters. It is likely that you'll meet many attractive prospects who won't be able to give you the time for much else. It's important for you to become a master of the Quick-Close. But don't worry, there will also be those times when you'll have the luxury of additional time for nurturing a conversation and developing that all-important chemistry.

When you have successfully mastered icebreaking, following up, and closing the deal, you'll have gained the remarkable ability to meet many prospects anywhere and at any time. This accomplishment will play a dramatic role in changing the status of your single life forever. It will propel you into an active social life with potentially fulfilling relationships around each and every corner. This reason alone should be motivation for you to become a master at closing the deal.

7

Using Three Winning Techniques

art I has covered just about every step in the general process of connecting with prospects. But before moving on to Part II, which offers ideas on where to go to find prospective love interests, make sure you familiarize yourself with three techniques that can be an asset to any successful plan for meeting someone special. These are the Seed-Planting Technique, the Laid-Back Technique, and the Use-of-Humor Technique.

SEED-PLANTING TECHNIQUE

Regardless of whether you see a prospect regularly or infrequently, you'll want that person to be aware that you find her desirable. Here's where you can implement the Seed-Planting Technique, which is a subtle way of letting people know you are attracted to them without making it seem like a come-on.

Simply plant little seeds of goodwill, friendliness, and mild attraction in the minds of your prospects. These "seeds" can range from a friendly hello that is accompanied by a nice smile and direct eye contact, to a pleasant line such as, "I'm lucky to have such a nice/pretty/handsome neighbor." Even a statement like, "You're my favorite cashier at this store," can plant a little seed of interest in that person. What you're really trying to communicate is that you like this person and find her attractive.

It is important to remember the names of prospects you have met casually and are attracted to. When you see them a second time, be sure to address them by their first name. Using your prospect's name sows a seed that she is important enough to remember. Most prospects will be flattered and impressed, especially if you don't see them often. People love when you remember their names. Also, remembering the name of a prospect's friend, roommate, family member, pet dog or cat will score big-time points for you as a thoughtful, caring person. Chances are that these are precisely the qualities that are important to your prospect.

If you legitimately cannot remember your prospect's name, you can say something like, "I forgot your name, but I didn't forget what you look like. My name is _____. What's yours?" This straightforward, honest statement will certainly get the other person's attention.

If your prospect responds positively, the seeds you have planted will grow naturally. Other times the seeds may require some degree of nurturing. And, of course, there will be those seeds that never mature due to any one of a number of reasons. Maybe the other person is already involved in a relationship or is simply not attracted to you. It is also possible that the person may have an attitude problem and may not be mentally capable of any romantic involvement. Such factors are beyond your control and should never discourage you from continuing your seed-planting efforts.

Bear in mind that the subtlety of this technique does work effectively. For the best chance at successful results, keep a positive attitude that is both kind and sincere when planting the seeds.

LAID-BACK TECHNIQUE

Some people find it very effective to approach prospects in a laid-back, nonaggressive manner, at least during the beginning of their quest to meet people. If you find yourself at a dance club or bar and don't feel comfortable with immediately (and maybe obviously) looking for someone special, the Laid-Back Technique—which takes a nonassertive approach—may be a better, more natural way for you to meet others.

Here's an example of how you can employ this technique at a dance club. Shortly after you enter the club, get yourself a drink and then find a comfortable seat in a highly visible area, such as close to the dance floor, at the bar, or near the entrance to the rest rooms. Now sit back and let the prospects check you out. If they're interested, they'll approach you.

Keep your eyes open for prospects who are either cruising near you or who have relocated to a spot in your vicinity. Chances are that these people have noticed you and want to get a better look. As with most approaches, but in particular with this one, be sure to make eye contact and smile to encourage prospects to get closer to you. If you're interested in a prospect who seems to have noticed you and has moved nearby, try an icebreaker. As the prospect has already shown some interest, you'll be amazed at how easy and natural it will be for you to deliver the line.

Furthermore, this approach allows you to appear easy-going, relaxed, and self-confident—qualities that will make you more attractive. By the way, don't be surprised if someone actually approaches you and attempts to break the ice first!

USE-OF-HUMOR TECHNIQUE

Humor wins hearts! Let's face it, we all like to laugh. Laughter is free, and it's one of life's greatest enjoyments. Why else are comedy clubs springing up all over the country? People usually enjoy your company if you can make them laugh. Humor can be disarming, as it helps a person relax and let down her guard. It is the ultimate icebreaker.

Of course, we're not prompting you to act like a clown or a cornball! What we are encouraging is that you become a fun person to be with by incorporating a little wit or humor into your personality. This will make the other person laugh or smile, and it lets her know that you enjoy talking to her.

Quick Wit

There are times when you can initiate humor through a blunt, flirty line. Let's say that you're working out in a fitness club and spot an attractive prospect who is also working out. First, make eye contact and smile. Then say something like, "I don't know what's better for my health—my exercising or my watching you exercise!" Of course, make sure you deliver the line with a big smile on your face. Hopefully, you'll get a laugh. And if a conversation happens to develop, who knows where it might lead! Below, several more approaches using humor are discussed.

Harmless Self Put-Downs

Another way of using humor to your advantage is by poking fun at yourself. If done properly, this technique lets a prospect know that although you can be serious, you don't take yourself too seriously. Always make sure that the put-downs are delivered in a light, humorous way. After all, you don't want to make yourself look like a fool!

Let's say you want to use a humorous (yet harmless) self put-down as an icebreaker. Try walking up to your prospect with sad-looking puppy-dog eyes. With an exaggerated sigh say, "Hello. I have no life. Please have pity and talk to me." Delivered properly, this icebreaker could cause that person to chuckle, at the very least.

Maybe you and a prospect are having a conversation about the different seasons. You might inject some humor by saying, "I love the summer even though I usually don't have good luck in hot weather. I get buzzed by bees, constantly burn my feet on the sand, and always manage to drip ice cream on whatever I'm wearing."

If you're discussing sports with a prospect, you might say something such as, "I'm interested in most sports, but I don't like going to baseball games. I've been to only two, but during those games I was hit in the head with a foul ball, needed oxygen due to the excessive heat and humidity at the stadium, and stained a perfectly good pair of jeans by sitting on some cotton candy that was stuck to my seat. It's safe to say that I can live without going to another baseball game. However, I'd be delighted to have you at my side at the football game on Sunday afternoon, provided I can bring along some protective gear!"

These examples show how you can humorously poke fun at yourself, yet still show a strong interest in getting together with your prospect. All it takes is a little creativity to incorporate this technique into your conversation.

Unexpected One-Liners

You can also use humor to your advantage by injecting a funny line at an unexpected but appropriate time, even if it may rationally *seem* to be during an inappropriate situation. For example, consider being in an elevator, a doctor's office, a dentist's office, or another place where soft background music is being played. If someone attractive is on the elevator or in such an office, you might say, "Excuse me, but would you care to dance? They're playing one of my favorites." You could accompany this line with arm and body motions that suggest dancing. The person will probably smile or break up laughing because your dance request is so absurd.

Here's an example of how humor helped break the ice for a gentleman who was attracted to the hostess of a restaurant he frequented. When she asked if he wanted the smoking or nonsmoking section, he first responded appropriately and then simply added, "And I'd like a table with an ocean view." Of course, there was no such view anywhere in the restaurant. She laughed and directed him to a table. During his meal, the hostess stopped by to see how he was enjoying the "view." At this point, he got her involved in a bit more conversation, and by the time he left the restaurant, he had her phone number.

Humor is a positive force. Most people would rather smile and chuckle than stare blankly ahead. And your humor muscles will strengthen with exercise, so use your humor often. Practice one-liners with friends and coworkers. If a joke really works, consider modifying it for use as an icebreaker. If you make your first impression memorable by causing an immediate amused reaction, you could simultaneously be creating a foundation for future laughing and loving with your new prospect.

A WORD TO THE WISE

As you find prospects and get to know them, continue to be warm and light-hearted. Sow seeds with sincerity, project an easy-going attitude, and whenever possible, get your prospect to smile or laugh.

By now you should have a handle on some basic strategies that are helpful for starting a romantic encounter. You've packaged yourself desirably, you've worked on your attitude, and you are psyched to get out there and meet people. So, what's the next step? It is determining where "out there" is, and knowing what to do when you get there. You are ready to move on to Part II of this book. It suggests specific avenues you can take to meet people, as well as particular places to go to find that certain someone. In addition, each section offers scores of icebreaking lines for you to use in specific situations.

PART TWO

Where to Meet Someone Special

There is a myriad of places and events where single people can meet other single people, and quite a few are mentioned throughout Part II. You're probably anticipating some of the locations and functions we'll be discussing, but others may surprise you. In fact, some of the suggestions might never even have crossed your mind as a "singles opportunity"—for example, camping clubs, health food markets, libraries, and yard sales. Keep an open mind and you'll be finding prospects in every direction!

For situations discussed, we'll include icebreaking lines that might be useful in the specific setting. Of course, the lines given are only the tip of the iceberg. They're really offered just to stimulate you to start thinking of your own lines. As with the lines suggested in Part I, you can and should modify them. Make sure that when you use a line, you feel comfortable saying it. Otherwise, it won't help you. In any situation, remember the two steps to meeting and developing a relationship with someone—break the ice, then follow up.

The message is clear—you can meet someone and start a romantic encounter just about anywhere! Yes, it requires effort, but it's definitely worthwhile. So let's discuss possible places and events where you can start moving in the right direction.

8

Singles Events—
Mixers and Meals

The various singles events and co-ed endeavors that you'll be reading about in this chapter are designed solely to bring singles together and are categorized as "singles oriented sites and functions." Many people laughingly refer to them as "singles dysfunctions." This may be because some people believe that a high number of dysfunctional individuals come to these events. But other, more enterprising singles find that these functions offer a wealth of opportunities for meeting prospects. Try some. What do you have to lose? Remember, you need only to connect with one special person.

The most common singles events are singles dances and singles parties. In many areas, there are also singles game nights. Finally, singles luncheons, dinners, barbecues, and dining clubs are available, if you like the thought of meeting over a plate of good food. Be sure to consider all your options.

SINGLES DANCES

Among the most popular functions for meeting prospects are singles dances. They occur in many different types of environments and take place year-round. They can be especially helpful for meeting prospects during the holiday season.

Singles dances have always been popular for bringing together large numbers of eager people. The best dances are the ones that are sponsored either by a religious organization or by a group that runs dances professionally. Let's discuss the former. You will be more apt to find someone of your own faith at a dance sponsored by a religious organization. If you're concerned about potential problems down the road involving religious beliefs and child rearing, this may be a good path to follow.

As mentioned above, there are also singles dances designed to draw a wider selection of prospects. Organizations sponsoring these dances place less emphasis on religious beliefs and more on bringing in healthy admission fees and packing the hall with singles. There is usually a big turnout and a great mix of people at these dances.

Many people meet and connect at singles dances, so these affairs should never be overlooked. However, if you're shy, you may feel uncomfortable approaching desirable prospects unless you have practiced and prepared beforehand. So spend the necessary time practicing your lines and preparing for a variety of reactions to your approach. But most of all, plan on having fun and enjoying the music!

Lines for Singles Dances

❏ "I'd really love to dance this one with you."

❏ "Could you save a slow dance for me?"

❏ "The turnout is fantastic tonight, isn't it?"

❏ "Every time I see you, you're wearing the same thing." (*This humorous line is for use with someone you've never seen before.*)

❏ "I didn't realize they were having a beauty pageant tonight. Where are the rest of the contestants?"

SINGLES PARTIES

Singles parties are a great way to meet attractive prospects. Some singles parties are run by local companies whose specific business is to sponsor these events, while others (such as the Meeting Group Party, which has its base in St. Louis, Missouri) are run by companies that sponsor parties across the nation. The admission fee for most singles parties is fifteen dollars or more, depending on whether food is served and what the actual nature of the event is. The parties are usually held at large hotels such as the Holiday Inn, Sheraton, or Hilton, which are easily accessible and have plenty of parking.

Theme Parties

Some singles parties have themes, and some are distinctive for the way the participants are encouraged to meet each other. For example, at one type of party, once your admission fee is paid, you are given a creative nametag, as well as a corresponding partner to seek out and start a conversation with. You may be Scarlett—according to your name tag—and you should find Rhett somewhere among the partygoers. Lucy would search for Desi, Fred would look for Ginger, Fric would seek out Frac, and so on. When you find your designated nametag partner (as well as any other prospects who seem appealing), you'll have the option of enjoying light conversation, dancing, eating, drinking, playing board games such as backgammon or checkers, or following the lead of the emcee in a fun game or activity.

The Meeting Group Party, mentioned on page 60, has a more sophisticated approach but still follows a central theme or direction. For your admission fee, you receive a nametag and a handful of small cards. On the front of the cards you write your first name and phone number, while on the back of the cards you check off appropriate printed messages. For example, you might find the following: "I enjoyed speaking with you; I'd like to speak with you some more," and "I didn't get a chance to talk to you but I'd like to. So here's my number; call me."

There are a couple of basic conditions to which all Meeting Group partygoers must adhere. You are not permitted to refuse a card from anyone. This is designed to eliminate any immediate and direct rejection. Also, you are advised to circulate. The emcee of the party, who keeps the event going and flowing, continually urges partygoers to keep meeting prospects for brief conversations of about five to fifteen minutes. During these short conversations, cards can be exchanged. This is a great way to meet everyone you find interesting.

Yet another twist at some singles parties is that you may be required to bring a guest of the opposite sex to the party. This insures a larger turnout of singles and also a more equal ratio of men to women.

Finally, "recycled date" theme parties have become another popular way of meeting new prospects. You can do one of these on your own. Speak with your friends, set a date, and enjoy a "leftover guys and gals" theme party at one of your homes. Ask everyone invited to bring a dish of food or dessert, wear a theme accessory—such as a hat or a Hawaiian or tie-dye shirt—and bring along a former date, prospect, or friend. "Recycled date" theme parties do not necessarily have to be formal, Saturday-evening types of affairs. You can plan them as casual

Sunday brunches instead. Either way, these parties are full of food, fun, festivities, and flirting.

Lines for Theme Parties

❑ "When I saw you, I felt compelled to mingle with you. I took advanced mingling in college."

❑ "If I can't mingle with you, I want my admission fee back."

❑ "There's a lot of people here, but I'm only concerned with talking to you. Do you mind?"

❑ "I would give you my birth certificate if I didn't have any cards left."

❑ "I love the way you wear your hat. You've got a great hat face."

❑ "Who did you come to the party with?"

❑ "What would you be doing now if you weren't at this party?"

❑ "What dish did you bring tonight/today?"

❑ "Can we sample each other's dishes?"

❑ "What are your feelings on being a recycled date?"

❑ "I'm a non-recycled friend and proud as punch. And your story?"

House Parties

Singles house parties are another way to meet interesting people. These kinds of parties, usually for a specific age range, are often advertised in local newspapers for particular dates and times. All you pay is a small cover charge at the door to reimburse the host for the food and drinks.

Singles house parties are informal get-togethers of motivated singles who generally do not like the club scene. They prefer, instead, to meet other unattached people in a casual, homey atmosphere. If you haven't tried a house party yet, you should definitely attend one. In addition, if you have the room—and the courage—throw your own house party.

Lines for Singles House Parties

❑ "This living room is wonderful! I feel like I'm home."

❑ "Would you like to take a look at the patio/backyard/balcony?"

❑ "This couch makes me feel like I'm sitting on a cloud."

❏ "Trade you!" *(This line should be said while offering the prospect some Hershey's Kisses.)*

Pool Parties

A swimming pool environment is another great place for singles to meet. Singles can get together to enjoy swimming at a daytime function that includes lunch and mingling. Or pool partygoers can gather in the evening, dressed casually and chatting poolside, with cocktails and munchies. With a backdrop of candlelit tables and a moonlight ambiance, nighttime pool parties make a very romantic setting in which to meet a special prospect.

Singles who enjoy swimming may also find prospects at their local public pool, college campus pool, or area swim club. More outdoor and athletic ideas are found in Chapter 13.

Lines for Singles Pool Parties

❏ "The moon, the pool, and you—what a romantic trio."

❏ "I love the way the moonlight is bouncing off your hair."

❏ "Can I get you a towel?"

❏ "Was your father a thief?" *(Wait for response.)* "Because he stole the stars right out of the sky and put them in your eyes."

This section covers the most common types of singles parties out there. But you should be creative and see what you can come up with! This is just a start.

SINGLES GAME NIGHTS

Singles game nights are a fun way to get out and meet prospects. Game nights involve a selection of activities including card games (such as pinochle, gin rummy, poker, and bridge), board games (such as backgammon, checkers, chess, Scrabble, and Monopoly), and other games (such as Yahtzee, ping pong, pool, and air hockey). Bingo nights, often held in churches or under other organizational sponsorship, also fit into this category.

The idea at singles game nights is to find an interesting prospect and to engage in any one of a number of games with that person, either individually or as part of a group. Game nights are wonderful for helping singles to connect with each other and also to establish a shared interest in specific games or activities. If you like playing cards or games and are looking for someone to share your life with, singles game nights are a must for you.

Lines for Singles Game Nights

❑ "Would you like to share this game with me?"

❑ "Would you be interested in being my partner for this game?"

❑ "We need another player for this game. Do you want to join us?"

❑ "I bet that spending time with you would be even more fun than this game."

SINGLES MEALS

Many good times are had when people share a meal. Whether at a small table, a banquet table, or a café counter, food brings people together. That's why there are a lot of singles events organized around meals.

Luncheons and Dinners

Singles luncheons and dinners are where hordes of singles spend from ten to twenty-five (or more) dollars to join other singles for a one-time meal. The quality of the food varies, depending upon the restaurant or caterer, but the food is not the purpose of the event. Go to a singles luncheon or dinner because you are hungry for a mate, not a meal. If the food is good, consider it a bonus.

Singles luncheons and dinners are often buffet-style, so that singles can eat what they want, when they want, and wherever they want. Here is a sure-fire, five-step method for successfully mingling, meeting, and dining at buffet-style affairs (this method can be used at other singles activities too):

1. Scan the room to find the prospects who appeal to you. Mentally target, in order of priority, the two or three prospects you most want to meet. If you see more than three very desirable prospects, keep the remainder as back-ups in case your first three prospects do not work out.

2. Sit down at the table of prospect number one, with only a first course such as a bowl of soup or a salad. Remember, if you intend to meet single prospects in this fashion, you must sit at their table, or at one nearby, to be able to strike up a conversation.

3. If prospect number one responds to you in a positive manner, after you go back to the buffet to get your next course, return to the same table to further the rapport. Or ask the prospect if he would like to join you at the buffet or if there is anything you could bring back. This will aid in developing a bond with your prospect.

4. If your attempts with prospect number one prove unsuccessful, no matter what the reason, return to the buffet for your next course but, with your plate of food in hand, go to the table of prospect number two. You can say, "Somebody took my seat at the other table. Is it okay if I pull up an empty chair here?" Or "You look interesting. I thought I'd join you for lunch/dinner." Or "Do you mind if I break bread with you?" Proceed as you did before—try to start a conversation, create a rapport, and develop some chemistry.

5. If you are unsuccessful with prospect number two, get more food or some dessert and coffee from the buffet, then go to prospect number three's table and proceed as before.

Incidentally, even if something positive develops with one prospect, you can still try to meet other people. Just ask for the first prospect's phone number and say that you look forward to speaking again soon. Excuse yourself, go back to the buffet for more food or dessert, then sit down at the table of a new prospect.

The purpose of buffet-style luncheons and dinners is twofold. Essentially, the buffet format allows you to meet as many prospects as possible, while also giving you a way out when you find yourself sitting with someone whom you realize you are not interested in or who has no interest in you. By the way, try not to take too much food each time you go to the buffet table or you'll find yourself stuffed very quickly!

In the unlikely event that the singles luncheon or dinner is not set up buffet-style, scan the room for your number-one choice of a prospect immediately upon entering so that you can get a seat in a good location. Then try your best to establish a rapport and make a connection either during or after the meal.

Lines for Singles Luncheons and Dinners

❑ "Isn't this great food?"

❑ "Which salad dressing would you recommend?"

❑ "What is that on your plate? It looks delicious!"

❑ "This clam chowder/roast beef/chocolate cake is wonderful! I highly recommend it."

Barbecues and Picnics

Singles barbecues and picnics are a fine way to get out and meet other singles during warm weather. They are frequently advertised in newspapers and magazines, not to mention local papers and church bulletins. Such events usually have a more than adequate turnout of single prospects. Combine a relaxing afternoon, the warm sun, and comfort food with the possibility of meeting a wonderful new person, and you've got a winning situation.

Lines for Singles Barbecues and Picnics

❑ "Can I get you a hot dog/hamburger/drink/napkin?"

❑ "I would be delighted to hold your ear of corn while you nibble."

❑ "I, along with the ants that are sharing my picnic table/blanket, would be very happy to have you join us."

❑ "Excuse me, but would you please allow me to protect you from any grasshoppers or bees with bad attitudes?"

Dining Clubs

Singles dining clubs are a terrific way to meet single prospects and, at the same time, dine out at some of the finer restaurants in your area. Single people have the opportunity to join other unattached people in enjoying elegant, exceptional, exciting, and exotic meals.

Membership in a singles dining club brings with it a wide array of monthly events. Some dining clubs also offer travel packages to cities around the United States or abroad for unique culinary experiences. If you like to eat, dining clubs are a great way to meet prospects.

Information on singles dining clubs can be obtained from singles newspapers and magazines, as well as from food and gourmet magazines, all of which are available at newsstands and bookstores. Also, look in the food or restaurant section of your local newspaper or in the listing of area singles activities.

Lines for Singles Dining Clubs

❑ "How long have you been a member of this club?"

❑ "How does this restaurant compare to others you've eaten at?"

❑ "Have you belonged to any other clubs?"

❑ "I don't know about you, but I feel fate has put our culinary appetites together."

❑ "Is there a club you can join where singles share indigestion problems from dining out?"

At meal-oriented singles events, conversation flows easily. The relaxed and social environment associated with sharing a meal puts everyone at ease. Seriously consider looking into various singles meal events in your area.

CONCLUSION

If you're not currently participating in any singles activities, you're passing up good opportunities to meet prospects. Singles get-togethers are specially designed to provide fun and the chance to meet other unattached people. By attending these kinds of functions and activities, you may develop a new interest or hobby, make a new friend, or, best of all, find the love of your life. And if you didn't find anything that appeals to you in this chapter, keep reading. Many additional singles services are available to you, starting with personal ads, which are discussed in Chapter 9.

9

Personal Ads—
Prospects in Print

*P*ersonal ads are still one of the hottest ways to meet prospects. Why? Because it's as easy as shopping for groceries. You look down a list of descriptions and pick what sounds good to you. There's lots of choice and *everyone* on the list is available. Many people would much rather advertise themselves in print or call someone who has done so. The initial contact will then be over the phone. Keep in mind that any time you try to meet other people, you're "selling" yourself, and some people feel very uncomfortable "selling" themselves in a face-to-face manner. Personal ads are a great option.

Let's face it. Some people are prejudiced against personal ads. They feel if someone has to advertise in print, she must not be doing too well in person. That's actually not true. There are many good-looking, intelligent people who place or respond to ads, some because they're too busy to go out as often as they feel they would need to, and others because they want to get to know a prospect before they go on a date. If you find yourself among the many who would consider using personal ads, read this chapter which discusses both placing personal ads and responding to them.

FINDING THE RIGHT PUBLICATION

The first step in using personal ads is to identify the local newspapers and magazines that run ads for singles. Make sure that you like the way the ads are displayed and the procedures that are used to place or respond to them. For example, assess the price for a decent sized ad. Confirm that the periodical provides a safe way for people to make initial communication. Some publications forward letters to the ad-placers, while others provide a central number through which you leave a message for the person whom you are interested in. Lastly, check that the periodical is reputable if it is unfamiliar to you.

Once you have selected the periodical you want to use, decide whether you prefer drawing up your own ad or responding to someone else's. Answering ads is simple and will get you started inexpensively. Responding to ads will be covered later in this chapter. Many people, however, find that it is more productive to write and place their own ads.

PLACING YOUR OWN AD

Personal ads take time and effort to write, as well as money to place. However, if you place your own ad you will be exposed to hundreds, possibly thousands, of singles who really liked the initial information they read on you. If your ad is written well, even a one-time placement may bring you dozens of replies, if not more.

Remember that a poorly written ad will bring poor results. It's imperative that you make your ad a winner in order to yield the best responses. Study the personals column for ideas. See which ads attract your attention. Then ask yourself what it is about those ads that caught your eye. Did they include sparks of creativity or humor? Did the ads emphasize certain traits, such as being family-oriented, polite, or professional?

There are helpful books on how to write personal ads. One good one is *How to Meet the Opposite Sex Through Personal Ads* by William F. Schopf (Plantation, FL: Fun in the Sun Publications, 1991). Another helpful book is *Personal Ads—Never Be Lonely Again* by Marlene C. Halbig (Laguna Beach, CA: Baron Publications, 1992). Both these books are very thorough in their discussion of how to write, place, and screen ads, and how to respond to them. For now, here are a few basic pointers regarding the preparation of personal ads:

- When writing a personal ad, be sure to list basic information about you, including age, sex, race, religion, and marital status.

- Include important physical characteristics (height, build, hair color, eye color) and personality qualities (sincerity, honesty, intelligence, sense of humor).

- List any significant "disqualifiers" (physical handicap, smoking) that might eliminate prospects.

- Include any interests and non-negotiables (see page 18) that you will not or cannot compromise on (children, pets, physical fitness activities).

- List what you are seeking in a respondent, including physical characteristics and personality qualities, and state what you do not want as well.

- Keep your ad short. A lengthy ad will not attract more responses. In fact, research has suggested that the opposite is true. In addition, even though you may want to include every detail about yourself and exactly what you're looking for in a prospect, the more general you keep your ad, the larger the number of respondents will be.

- Be sure to use the publication's specific code. Abbreviations are used for terms such as single, divorced, Christian, Jewish, and gay, just to name a few. In the following section, you will find a key to the abbreviations that are most commonly used in many periodicals, but not all periodicals use the same exact ones.

The latest trend in personal ads is twenty-four-hour voice mail service. You can have a voice-mail box number assigned to your personal ad, so that anybody interested in your ad can phone the voice-mail box number and hear a recorded greeting from you. People usually like hearing voices. The phone greeting can be something as simple as the reading of your personal ad, or it can be completely different and creative—maybe a reading of your favorite poem or even the singing of a short song!

People can usually call the publication's special telephone number to browse through many different voice ads. If they find any that interest them, they can punch in the voice-mail box number and leave a message, their name, and their telephone number. Those who place ads call in daily or weekly to check their messages.

The wonderful thing about writing—and perhaps recording—a personal ad is that you can advertise for exactly the type of person you would like to meet. Also, due to the high numbers of people who read personal ads, you may receive a good number of qualified prospects. You can get many replies from just one well-written personal ad, so it may be worth a try.

DECODING THE PERSONALS

Half the fun of reading personal ads is trying to decipher the string of abbreviations that starts them off. You must learn exactly what each abbreviation means in a given periodical. In addition, be sure to proofread your own ad several times to confirm that you are communicating the right message. After all, you *are* writing in code.

The following list provides some of the more common abbreviations used in today's publications. But remember that the codes publications use for personal ads vary. Therefore, the periodical that you select might use a somewhat different system or have additional abbreviations.

M	Male	H	Hispanic	NM	Never married
F	Female	L	Lesbian	J	Jewish
B	Black	BI	Bisexual	C	Christian
W	White	S	Single	NR	Not religious
G	Gay	D	Divorced	NS	Nonsmoker
A	Asian	WW	Widowed	ISO	In search of

HANDLING RESPONSES TO YOUR AD

When you get responses to your ad, your first step should be to separate the letters or messages sent by those individuals you feel are potentially interesting from the responses of those you have absolutely no wish to meet. Evaluate how desirable each prospect seems.

If you are dealing with letters, you might want to divide your letters into three categories: Category "A" could contain those respondents who seem genuinely interesting—people you intend to contact. Category "C" could contain those people you definitely will not contact. Logically, Category "B" would then be for those people you are not sure about but haven't yet eliminated; putting them in a "hold" category lets you defer the decision until a later time.

Some ad-placers never have to turn to category "B," either because they have so many "A" respondents or because they hit it off with somebody in category "A" rather quickly. However, if you have met everyone in your "A" group and have not yet been successful, you can return to the "B" group, re-evaluate the respondents, and follow up accordingly.

If you are retrieving phone messages from the voice-mail account you have with the periodical, take notes as you listen to the messages.

Then categorize your prospects as described in the above discussion on letter responses.

Once you decide whom you would like to meet, it's up to you to make the contact. Make your phone conversation simple. Identify yourself by your first name. Mention that you had an ad in the personals and give the name of the publication. You can restate the ad, if you desire, to jog your prospect's memory. Try to get a light conversation going.

With basic and friendly questions like those listed below, your prospect should not have any trouble holding up the other end of the conversation. If the prospect mentioned something interesting or unusual in her letter or message, ask about it. The more interested you act in your prospect, the more interested your prospect will be in meeting you.

By the way, if you get an answering machine the first time you call a respondent, *do not* leave your name or telephone number. Why? You may decide that you do not want this person to have your telephone number, so why leave it?

Lines for Your First Phone Conversation

❑ "Have you ever used the personals before?"

❑ "Do you read the newspaper/magazine often?"

❑ "You sound so interesting. I want to know more. What else can you tell me?"

❑ "What type of things do you like to do on a first date?"

RESPONDING TO AN AD

If you decide to respond to an ad rather than to write your own, remember that the person who placed the ad will probably receive numerous replies. You'll want your reply to stand out. There are a few things you should keep in mind to accomplish this:

If Writing a Letter

• Use colorful paper or even a colorful envelope. This may seem trivial, but it makes your response stand out immediately.

• Make sure that you either use very neat handwriting or type your letter. One of the biggest turnoffs is a sloppily written response.

- Send out freshly typed letters to each ad you respond to. Another big turnoff is receiving a photocopied response—obviously one of a batch sent out to respond to several ads.

If Leaving a Message Through the Publication

- Use your authentic voice. If you tend to have a squeaky or loud voice, you might be tempted to change it to something raspy or smooth. While a sexy sounding voice might catch someone's attention, you are bound to break into your "real" voice later on. So you might as well not pretend. If you naturally have a raspy or smooth voice, that's a different story.

- Speak slowly and clearly enough so that the listener can grasp your information and write down your number. Avoid starting off on the wrong foot by forcing the person to replay your message three times just to get your name and number straight.

- Always be polite and respectful. Be aware that the listener cannot see your facial expressions or body language. Therefore, consider practicing your message beforehand, making sure there is no way to interpret it as sarcastic or too weird.

For Both

- Keep your response succinct but include some enticing details.

- Make sure that you respond to the wording of the ad rather than just composing a form letter or common message. If nothing in your response focuses on the specific ad, it may appear that you're responding to many different ads with the same reply. A good response addresses the key words, thoughts, goals, and requested characteristics in the ad.

- Be creative. Nothing is worse than a boring, run-of-the-mill response. Try a unique approach, such as humor—but not too corny, please!

- Whether in writing or via voice, sound enthusiastic about meeting the person, but don't sound like you're begging! Sound confident, intelligent, and charming!

If you offer an interesting, positive response, you hopefully will soon hear from the placer of the ad. In your telephone conversation, be as natural and sure of yourself as possible. As with any other technique described in this book, using the personals is a skill, one that you can refine through practice. If you have success right away, great! But if not, don't give up. Learn from your efforts, polish your techniques, and look forward to meeting many more wonderful people.

ARRANGING A MEETING

If you get along with the prospect during your telephone conversation(s), you are likely to plan a date. Arrange the initial meeting in a public place; make sure you meet on neutral territory. You don't want to invite a stranger to your home, even if it's just to pick you up, and you certainly don't want to go to a stranger's home! Why? Simply because you may decide that you do not want this person to know where you live. By meeting in a busy public place, you'll feel safe.

Good locations for first meetings are coffee shops and diners. Bear in mind that the purpose of this initial meeting is to see if there is any chemistry between you and your prospect. And remember that you are not obligated to do anything with anyone you have no interest in.

Also, when you arrange the initial meeting, make sure that each of you knows what the other person looks like or will be wearing. It can be very embarrassing to have to wait for a total stranger to approach you and timidly ask your name, or for you to have to do the same. If you wear something unusual, such as a flower or a cap or a brightly colored scarf, it can make identification much easier and can also be an icebreaker in a situation that many people find awkward.

DECLINING FURTHER CONTACT

Trust your instincts. You may find that you're uncomfortable with the person you're talking to or meeting with. Don't try to convince yourself that, because of one particular positive characteristic, you should disregard your gut feeling.

There's nothing wrong with ending an initial contact or meeting with an open-ended promise such as, "Let me see how I feel in a few days," or "Give me some time to think about this, and then we'll talk some more." Don't feel obligated. If it doesn't seem to be working out, there's no reason to prolong the agony. Simply say, "Thank you very much for meeting with me, but I don't think this would work." As with other lines, practice until you feel confident and comfortable.

If you're not completely sure that you want to meet a prospect again, but you're not ready to strike the person off your list, you may want to set up another "public" meeting. A second meeting may help you to solidify your feelings.

CONCLUSION

At the very least, the personal ads are a great way to check out how people promote themselves. And if you have decided to give them a try, personal ads are a fun way to contact many potential dates. As long as you take proper precaution, "prospect" intelligently, and have realistic expectations, using the personal ads is a very valid way to enhance your social life.

10

The Internet— Cyber-Meeting and Cyber-Dating

*C*urrently, the most popular way to meet other singles is over the internet. The reason for this is that you don't have to set foot outside the comfort of your own home to find qualified prospects. Also, responses can be immediate and plentiful. The icing on the cake is that the cost of cyber-dating is minimal, making it affordable for just about everyone who is single and looking for romance, a relationship, or friends.

Literally hundreds of thousands of photos with profiles of men and women can be found at the click of a mouse. You can specify preferences encompassing age, religion, ethnicity, sexuality, and locality, which may be specific to a city, state, or country. And even more specific data can be found on an individual's personal profile, often including weight, height, hair and eye color, interests, compatibility, degree of education, employment status, marital status, interest in pets, smoking status, type of lifestyle, and much more. Cyber-dating provides you with the opportunity to learn a lot about a person before a face-to-face meeting takes place. Cyber-introductions—or "cyber first dates"—provide singles the opportunity to share their innermost feelings from their hearts, minds, and souls while in the comfort of their own homes.

FINDING SITES ON THE INTERNET

Online personal sites are easy to find on the internet. A search will return literally hundreds of cyber-dating sites, but only a few good ones will stand out. Select a site that is reputable, that keeps your e-mail confidential and doesn't allow profanity or off-color jokes. That way, you'll feel free to be yourself when interacting with other members. It's always best to use a site that your friend or another reliable source has recommended.

Sites that require payment generally provide an environment where the users are more committed to finding a partner than unpaid sites. Take special note of the payment procedures though. Some sites require a monthly membership fee that usually ranges from ten to fifty dollars. Others ask for an annual fee. Still others request a large but one-time fee. Yet another type has you purchase credits on a site that can be redeemed for fee-based services. These services are usually two to five dollars each, with minimum quantities required at the time of purchase. Whatever the case, in order to correspond with or contact a prospect, there is usually some kind of fee involved. All sites accept credit cards as the preferred method of payment.

A good idea is to explore dating sites that cater to your specific interests, religion, or lifestyle. For example, Jdate.com is for Jewish singles, eharmony.com is for Christian singles, and gay11.com is for gay singles. You should also explore cyber-dating sites with well-known reputations, such as Match.com, Etroductions.com, Udate.com, Kiss.com, LavaLife.com, Datadate.com, and MatchMaker.com. Once you find a site that stands out above the rest—and one that suits your financial situation—go ahead and subscribe.

PREPARING YOUR PROFILE

After finding and joining a site you feel safe and comfortable with, the next step is filling out the profile questionnaire. It's wise to answer each question or option available on the questionnaire. Your answers will give people a better sense of who you are, as well as some points of discussion when you eventually begin to communicate with another member of the service.

Filling out profiles are a wonderful opportunity for real self-discovery and will inspire you to look inward at what you have to offer. Before you actually enter your profile online, take time to assess how you feel about yourself. What are your best and worst qualities, your interests, your desires, and your values? Write down your thoughts. Read them, add to them, and then begin your profile.

It is best to be completely honest in your profile. Being open about yourself can be a bit frightening, but the right person will desire you just the way you are. When you get to know a person, the truth will come out anyway, so honesty is always best.

A point to remember is that nothing will turn off online prospects more than a flurry of spelling mistakes in your profile. Be sure that everything you enter is correctly spelled. If necessary, type it on a word processor with spell-check to insure proper spelling.

Most successful profiles contain an eye-catching headline. Your headline is a one-sentence statement about yourself or what you are searching for. Funny or catchy headlines are more likely to entice people to view the entire profile. So feel free to exercise your witty sense of humor while arranging your profile.

In order to receive responses, you will need to establish an e-mail account specifically for internet dating. Select a screen name that best identifies your personality without going over the edge. Be creative and charming!

We all know that a picture is worth a thousand words. A current photo of you at your most pleasing will boost responses to your profile. Most cyber-dating sites will encourage you to provide a photo. You can use a digital camera, a scanner, or simply bring your best photo(s) to a local copy center such as Staples or Office Depot and ask them to scan it onto a floppy disk for you. It's a known fact that many people will search only for profiles with photos. So truthfully, photos are a must. You might as well not prolong the inevitable; provide the photo up front. Consider the fact that you can use your photo to tell more about you. If you tend to be a bubbly person, a photo of you wearing your broad smile will make you seem more approachable and generate more responses. If you are an animal lover, submit a photo of you nuzzling up to your pet. That will draw other animal lovers to you.

Another unique way to enhance the probability of prospect response is the addition of your own voice-bytes. More and more online dating sites are offering this interesting feature. A voice-byte is an uploaded vocal version (up to five minutes) of your best and most charming thoughts and ideas. Voice-bytes provide one more piece of ammunition in the cyber-dating arsenal.

Your personal profile is your piece of advertising. Make it as attractive and informative as possible. Moreover, update your profile whenever you have something new to say about yourself. Did you finish your degree? Did you accept a new job? Do you have a new interest in travel?

Make sure your profile does you justice and tracks all of your personal progress.

SEARCHING FOR COMPATIBLE MATCHES

There would not be much value to a cyber-dating site if it did not provide a search function. The concept of the search function is that it allows you to enter information on the type of person you are interested in meeting, and then it highlights those members who match your compatibility requirements. The best search functions are ones that allow you to submit specific geographic locations; you can limit your search to people who live within a specific distance from where you live.

Key features of good cyber-dating search functions are the ability to save a specific compatibility match and the opportunity to have new matches automatically e-mailed to you. These become huge time-saving features for busy cyber-daters who do not want to log in and go through a brand new search every time. In addition, some internet dating sites not only provide the capacity to search for romantic prospects, but also allow you to search for friends with common interests. For example, you can enter an ongoing search for dating prospects, as well as a search for tennis partners.

CORRESPONDING WITH SITE MEMBERS

After you have selected a member you would like to meet, use your cyber-dating site to contact him. Until you choose to reveal your identity to a cyber-dating prospect, your identity will remain anonymous. You will be known only by the screen name you have selected. To their great credit, cyber-dating sites will do everything possible to protect your identity, as they respect the value of anonymity.

One form of anonymous communication is through double blind e-mails. This form of correspondence allows you to communicate from your normal e-mail account but eliminates all identifying information and reformats it so that it hails from your "handle" or screen name at the cyber-dating site. Your prospect's reply will also appear to come from the site. But the e-mails are actually being forwarded to your usual e-mail account. The advantage is that there is only one e-mail account for you to check when retrieving correspondence from cyber prospects *and* your regular e-mail friends.

Many cyber-dating sites provide a built-in messaging center that can be used to correspond anonymously with other members. The advantage here is that you use this service to keep your dating-related e-mails from mixing with your usual e-mails on your home account. In other words, you maintain your personal e-mail account as usual, and you use the particular site's communication center for any correspondence between you and other members. An added plus is that it provides optimal integration between members and messages; there are links so that you can click your mouse on a member's name, for example, to view his online profile. There is also instant messaging between members.

Some cyber-dating sites have anonymous chat group programs. Even though it's not the best way to meet prospects, it can be an exceptional way to speak with a group of people and pass the time. If you can coordinate a time to "chat" with a specific member, communication can be much quicker than corresponding back and forth via e-mails.

Now, how do you break the ice when you actually have your first cyber-conversation with a prospect? Creating the perfect opening line or icebreaker can be very difficult. Considering the fact that, at this initial stage, your message could make or break your chance of a response, significant time should be devoted to crafting the appropriate icebreaker. Online icebreaking is an area where sincerity wins out over being cute.

Select one feature of your prospect's online profile that is of particular interest to you and feature it in the "subject" line of your e-mail. For example, "I love rock-climbing too," "Let's jam on our guitars," or "We could skydive on weekends." Within the body of your message, discuss some of the prospect's interesting features from his profile and why you find him appealing. Then mention the reasons why you feel the two of you could be compatible.

Try to keep your initial e-mail somewhat short, yet alluring. Provide ample information to arouse the prospect's curiosity and get him to check out your online profile. Hopefully, this will lead to a response. Your likelihood of a response depends upon the skill with which you created the icebreaking message and whether or not the prospect finds your online profile interesting.

To maximize your cyber-dating replies, seek out sites that permit no-charge correspondence. Some cyber-dating sites charge members to reply, which dramatically lowers your response rate. These dating sites should be avoided.

For the most part, if you select prospects who you feel are very likely to be compatible matches, you can expect about a twenty-five percent—or one-out-of-four—response rate from prospects that return the interest. As mentioned in Part I, always remember that it's a numbers game and there are plenty of prospects out there for you to contact. Hang in there; do not quit.

It's important to tend to responses within a one-week period. If you're not interested, a simple "Thank you, but I'm unable to communicate with you at this time" will be adequate. And for those who you continue to e-mail, try to personalize subsequent messages by responding to things mentioned in earlier e-mails and the online profile. Also, keep in mind that some people find it difficult to convey their true personalities upon initial contacts. So give people a chance by allowing them a few e-mails. Your hastiness could turn away a prospect who is a potential diamond in the rough.

It's also important not to e-mail someone obsessively, spilling the beans about your entire life story and bombarding him with messages. Try to leave interesting experiences and your life's tidbits for when you meet. Always be polite with everyone and treat all contacts the way you would want to be treated.

If humor is part of your everyday personality, certainly feel free to use it. But you must use humor carefully, as it's difficult to determine how the recipient is responding—humor doesn't always translate well over the internet. Finally, be sure to begin and end your e-mail with good etiquette. That means starting all e-mails with a greeting: "Dear _____,"; "Hello!"; "Whassup?" End all e-mails with a closing: "Regards"; "Sincerely"; "Best Wishes"; "Later"; or "Toodles." Don't forget to type in your handle, on-line name, or first name at the place where your signature would go in a hand-written letter.

Remember that the object of cyber-dating is to find someone who is close to what you're looking for, to arrange a telephone conversation, to schedule a one-on-one meeting, and eventually to go on a "real" first date if everything goes as planned. Nature will take its course from there.

GATHERING PRACTICAL POINTERS

Can you use a few more pointers when it comes to cyber-dating? Below, several common concerns are addressed in regard to internet dating sites. Let's start with how many sites you should join, and then move on to final precautions and healthy expectations.

Joining Multiple Sites

It's always best for singles to explore as many sites as possible and find one that feels exceptionally comfortable prior to subscribing to a cyber-dating site. Dedicate your time and efforts to being proactive in this area. In other words, do your research! There is no reason to spend a lot of money and experience a lot of aggravation due to membership with many sites. Using multiple sites may require too much energy—effort that could be channeled into finding and keeping your ideal match. In addition, you may lose track of whom you have contacted, not being able to remember what site a particular person is a member of. It is not recommended to have varying profiles on different sites.

So look around and only settle on a site that you feel very confident about. If it gives you a quality return on your investment of time, stick with it. If, after a few months, you are not happy with your response rate, certainly explore other sites.

Taking Precautions

Your safety and security are of paramount importance, and common sense is one's best safety measure with cyber-dating. Don't give out any personal information such as your place of work, last name, e-mail address, home address, or phone number until your instincts tell you that this is someone you can trust. Discontinue communications with anyone who tries to coerce you into revealing personal information by pressure or trickery.

Remember, it's always good to take your time. Often it's difficult to get a sense of a person's values and ethics from just a few e-mails. Go at your own pace. Ask a lot of questions and be on the alert for any inconsistencies, strange behavior, and for anyone who seems too good to be true. Now is the time to be a skeptic. E-mails can be very deceiving so don't get carried away in e-mail fantasy and fall in love at the click of a mouse. Wait until you meet before you fall head-over-heels in love. And please be sure to see a photo and talk on the phone before you meet.

It is wise to meet in an open, public place, such as a familiar coffee shop or restaurant, where there are plenty of people around. First meetings are best during the day, but this is not always possible. Provide your own transportation to and from the meeting and, if possible, always carry a cell phone. Never accept a ride with a stranger. Bring enough money to be prepared to pay for your own expenses. Tell a friend where you're going, when you expect to return, and the name, phone number, and e-mail address of the person you're meeting. Then, check in with your friend when you return.

Another idea is to bring a friend along or have him be at the meeting location at the same time but at a different table. Your friend can keep an eye on you and your date.

Plan for a short first meeting with a fixed time limit. For instance, agree to meet for coffee, a drink, or lunch. This way, there is no question about when the meeting will end. An ideal time limit for a first meeting is one to two hours. At the appropriate time, thank your date for meeting you and then say goodbye. If you determine that you like your prospect and want to see him again, make plans for future dates with a more extended period of time together. If you're pushed to stay longer, made to feel uncomfortable, or asked to compromise at any time, you have an easy way out and then you'll know right away that this is certainly not the person for you.

When you are meeting someone outside your local area and are flying in from another city, always arrange for your own hotel accommodations, car rental, and, if possible, carry a cell phone. Never permit your prospect to make the travel arrangements and do not identify the name of the hotel at which you are staying. When you arrive at the meeting location, assess it. Does it appear unsafe or unsuitable? If so, return to the hotel. At the hotel, attempt to contact your prospect at the location, on his cell phone, or at his home number. As always, use good judgement and be sure that a friend or family member is aware of your plans and has contact information in order to reach you.

In the event that you are uncomfortable or in any way frightened by your prospect, do your best to tactfully end the meeting and promptly leave the situation. If you feel you are in danger, simply excuse yourself from the table, saying that you need to call a friend or to ask someone at the location for assistance, and then slip out the back door and drive away, or even call the police. As always, your safety should be a top priority.

Assessing Hopes and Expectations

Like other aspects of one's life, your cyber-dating success ratio depends upon the effort you put in. If you are proactive and committed to forming a lasting relationship, then your chance of success is great. Successful dating, whether online or off, is defined differently by different people. Some marry, some build friendships that will last a lifetime, others expand their social circles and their social skills and eventually meet that special someone. The key is to have reasonable expectations and take it in stride if a relationship doesn't pan out. You can't take it personally. It just wasn't meant to be.

Acknowledging the Pitfalls

Some of the pitfalls of cyber-dating are that you risk choosing the wrong person and having your heart broken. But that's a pitfall of all dating. What pitfalls are relatively exclusive to internet singles sites?

If you're not careful about your security, you risk being in a difficult situation. People can hide behind the anonymity of the internet and then turn out to be insensitive or even unstable. Over e-mail, you risk having someone write terrible things to you because he thinks he can be abusive for fun. Additionally, you risk getting sexually inappropriate e-mails that are offensive.

You risk the investment in time and effort communicating with someone for an extensive amount of time, creating e-mail and phone fantasy, only to have your fantasy bubble burst when you meet your cyber-date and there is no chemistry. One of the major pitfalls of cyber-dating is that you cannot get a physical feel for the person with whom you are corresponding. Since chemistry is what makes it all happen, all of your shared common interests and desires are meaningless if chemistry is nonexistent when you meet your cyber-contact.

Finally, men complain that they receive very few responses from women and that many of their genuine and friendly e-mail inquiries yield no response whatsoever. If you are a man, you might want to put the effort forth anyway, as you never know when that one special lady will write back. Both sexes deal with prejudice against certain appearances when a prospect puts a lot of value in an internet photo. Your ad is likely to be instantly ignored if you don't show a photo, but it may be breezed over if you aren't good-looking enough in a photo. Again, these are problems that you should be aware of, but they are certainly not insurmountable if you are open to an internet singles search.

Despite the pitfalls and cautions, the internet is a great way to learn about countless singles. You should especially consider this option if you have a very busy work life and do not have a lot of time to go "prospecting" on your own, or if your local area lacks good singles functions. It's also generally fun to see who is out there, and the privilege of doing so from your own home is definitely tempting. As long as you take proper precaution and maintain a healthy attitude, you should be just fine!

CONCLUSION

Now that you have the lowdown on internet dating, you should get online and start looking at a few sites. It's important not to register with any site until you feel absolutely comfortable with the idea. Talk to other singles about their experiences and research lots of services. Register when you are ready. Many people are finding that the internet has helped to enhance their dating life, and you might find that cyber-romance is a great way to begin your next relationship.

11

More Singles Services—Turbo-Dating to Travel Clubs

*Y*ou might think we've covered all possible events and activities associated with specific singles functions. Not yet! There are several more options to consider before moving on to a wider perspective. You've certainly heard about singles dating clubs and video dating services, where you provide material for clients to review and possibly follow up on. You may or may not have heard about Turbo-Dating or Speed-Dating events—a newer, yet increasingly popular dating service. Finally, before venturing into the next few chapters, we'll discuss travel ventures specifically designed for groups of singles.

SINGLES CLUBS AND VIDEO DATING SERVICES

Some people join a singles dating club and/or video dating service to get "professional" help with their dating search. Singles dating clubs and video dating services are not for everyone, however. While some singles like the precise, high-tech methods used, others feel that microchips and videotapes take the romance out of dating. You need to decide for yourself if a computerized approach is for you.

Singles dating clubs and video dating services basically have the same approach. Both offer you the opportunity to meet other members who have been matched up with you according to comprehensive physical and psychological profiles. Depending on your budget, a membership or renewal can be very costly, though, and may net you only a few telephone numbers. On top of the somewhat hefty costs, some of the phone numbers may be for people who reside too far away from you to make a dating relationship feasible. So be sure to assess your financial situation to confirm that this type of service is the best way to go. You might call your local Better Business Bureau or Chamber of Commerce to verify that the club or service is legitimate and a quality enterprise. Ask your friends, too, if they know anyone who has ever belonged. If you have some extra money, it very well could be worth a shot!

What's the difference between the two? Video dating services go one step beyond singles dating clubs. In addition to using a computer to match you up with other members, video dating services also give you an opportunity to view firsthand what your prospects look like. The service is often expensive, but wouldn't it be worthwhile if you met your mate for life through one of those videos?

One firm that has had considerable success with its video dating program is Great Expectations. It has various programs available, but its standard "until married" membership is the most popular. Great Expectations offers members the freedom to make their own selections, whereas many other video dating services do the selecting for members. By making your own designations, you are in total control of who you meet and, at the same time, you remain anonymous until a choice is made.

At Great Expectations, the selection process starts by reviewing alphabetical listings of members, segregated by sex. Typed profiles and photographs of the members are kept in A-through-Z looseleaf binders. All the participants are identified by their first names and membership codes only, which are cross-referenced to their videos. It may take several office visits to go through all of the notebooks and to select the videos you wish to view.

The video profiles on the members are short but sweet. From the five-minute video, you should be able to decide if you have any further interest in a prospect. If you are interested, Great Expectations will send a postcard to the person indicating that another member would like to meet her. The selected prospect can then visit the Great Expectations office to examine your typed profile and video. If the member you chose is interested in you, too, Great Expectations will then give her your phone number to initiate contact. If the member you selected is not interested in you, you would not be contacted.

By the way, if you are interested in dating services but unable to afford them, you should consider getting a part- or full-time sales, marketing, or clerical job with a dating firm. Not only would you put money in your pocket, but you would also be exposed to genuine and sincere prospects while in your work environment. Also, if you wished to join the dating service, you would probably get an employee's discount off the normal membership or application fee!

Lines for First Contact Through a Singles Club or Video Dating Service

❑ "Our profiles show that we share a lot of interests. But tell me something about you that is not on your profile."

❑ "You looked really great in your video. And now you sound great in person."

❑ "I'm so happy that we agreed to make personal contact. I enjoy talking one-to-one."

SPEED-DATING/TURBO-DATING

An exciting new venue for rapidly evaluating many potential prospects in one evening has burst onto the singles scene. It's called Speed-Dating or Turbo-Dating, and this dating craze is sweeping large metropolitan cities and seducing singles searching for love.

As the name implies, this high-speed supersonic dating-at-the-speed-of-light option offers singles the opportunity to connect through one-on-one, sit down, mini blind dates. Individual mini-dates may last anywhere from three to eight minutes, and the number of mini-dates per event generally ranges from seven to twenty-five or more—depending upon the event organizer.

Some Speed-Dating organizers provide questionnaires to be completed by participants in advance. This additional feature enables participants to Speed-Date prospects who meet their pre-established qualifications related to age, interests, religion, education, ethnicity, sexual preference, and more. Speed-Dating organizers hold these mating marathon events at cafes, coffeehouses, nightclubs, restaurants, synagogues, churches, and auditoriums. The events fill up quickly.

The appeal of Speed-Dating is that it allows you to quickly assess the amount of chemistry and physical attraction—the critical components that are significant factors in the beginning stages of the dating process—between you and a prospect. Chemistry and physical attraction are necessary in order for two people to connect and want to get together again.

Speed-Dating is also popular because you avoid lengthy disastrous blind dates. You are meeting singles who already desire meeting someone, you meet in a pressure-free environment, the cost is generally less than the cost of one date, and you get to meet as many as twenty-five different prospects in one evening. It's also ideal for people who lack the time or resources to go out and meet other singles.

One firm, First Impressions of Cherry Hill, New Jersey, has found success with a maximum of twenty-eight people meeting in one evening. It works out to two groups of fourteen singles, with seven women and seven men per group. Each Turbo-Date lasts for seven minutes. First Impressions finds small, intimate groups to be much more comfortable for speed-daters than a room filled with hundreds of singles. Keep in mind that it's not important whether you meet seven or thirty-seven prospects in one evening; what is most important is that you *are* meeting new people.

Participants must follow certain rules when Speed-Dating. You are not permitted to ask anyone if she would like another date. You are not permitted to ask anyone for their telephone number, e-mail address, home address, last name, age, business card or any other contact information. You are not permitted to ask sexually explicit questions, use lewd language, or utter anything that could possibly be interpreted as threatening or sexual harassment.

Here's how it works. An equal number of men and women meet at a designated location that has been reserved for the event. All participants are given nametags with their first names, assigned seats, and dating forms. The place is filled with numbered tables for two. At the designated time, a man and a woman are assigned to one of the tables where they are allotted a specific amount of time to speak with one another. Each person then writes the name of the person they are speaking with onto their dating form.

Speed-Daters are given suggested topics to help generate conversation and to break the ice. Here are some popular questions to start and keep the conversation going: "Where did you grow up?" "What kind of work do you do?" "What is your ideal date?" "What kind of music do you like?" "Do you have any hobbies?" "Do you play or follow any sports?" "What's your favorite movie?" "What would be your perfect vacation?" "Do you plan on having children in the future?" The suggested topics and questions are designed to help singles learn information about what the potential prospects are really like. Hopefully, that information will enable them to decide if they would like to date that person again.

At the end of the designated amount of talk time, an event coordinator rings the bell and all mini-dates end. Once the bell has sounded, regardless of how engrossing the conversation is, participants are asked to fill out their dating forms indicating whether or not they have an interest in getting to know the person better on a less speedy date.

Once the dating forms have been filled in, the women remain seated and the men are required to rotate to the next table where another woman waits. The bell rings again and the next mini-date begins. Oftentimes midway through the event, there's a ten to fifteen minute break where participants can use the restrooms, get refreshments, and mingle before returning and completing all the mini-dates.

When the mini-dates are completed and the Speed-Dating event ends, participants are asked to submit their completed secret ballot dating forms to the event coordinators. The event coordinators then contact the participants via e-mail or telephone within forty-eight hours if both sides checked off the yes box, to provide phone numbers to those who want to get to know each other better.

At this point, life takes its normal course. Men and women who have matched up contact one another. The matched pairs begin dating. Many happily join the increasing number of singles who are becoming engaged and married through Speed-Dating events. For more information on Speed-Dating, you can read *Speed Dating: The Smarter, Faster Way to Lasting Love* by Yaacov Deyo and Sue Deyo.

Lines for Speed-Dating Events

❏ "Have you ever attended a Speed-Dating/Turbo-Dating event before?"

❏ "Do you know of anyone that has met someone through Speed-Dating?"

❏ "What do you do when someone that you've speed-dated previously and didn't connect with reappears in your new Speed-Dating group?"

❏ "I hope tonight's Speed-Dating event doesn't cause me to get a speeding ticket on the way home."

❏ "You're the type of person I'd like to slow date with after a speed-date."

TRAVEL

Who says that the best place to meet singles is at the popular local hang-outs? There are many wonderful opportunities to meet singles if you like to travel. Sometimes the reduced pressure when you are away from the hustle and bustle of your normal activities can increase your chances of making new relationships flourish.

Singles Weekend Get-Aways

Singles weekend get-aways are an option available to single people who want to get away from their surroundings for a combination mini-vacation and opportunity to meet other singles. There is generally a wide range of carefully planned activities available to help introduce participants. All you have to do is get involved in any activity that interests you, and you will meet prospects.

Singles weekend get-aways are a lot of fun, but they are still just a vacation. Enjoy them as such, and try not to have any further expectations. If you are lucky, you will meet someone who lives within train or cruise-control distance of your hometown.

Lines for Singles Weekend Get-Aways

❑ "Where did you hear about this trip?"

❑ "Have you ever gone on a get-away before?"

Singles Vacations

Another opportunity to be considered is the singles vacation—a longer version of the weekend get-aways. Singles vacations generally range anywhere from four nights and five days to two full weeks. They are booked by travel agencies and usually offer a variety of exciting vacation spots around the world as the destination. Examples of travel packages and programs that cater to the whims and needs of single people are Club Med and Hedonism, although there are many other programs available, too.

Singles vacation programs offer unattached people the opportunity to spend their travel time having fun with other singles. The only possible drawback is that these trips are booked by singles from all over the country—and maybe the world. Therefore, you may very well meet and share some quality time with a prospect who actually lives too far away from you. If you would consider a long-distance relationship, however, go for it! Singles vacations can be a great way to spend your vacation time.

Lines for Singles Vacations

❑ "Have you ever come to one of these resorts before?"

❑ "All of a sudden, this vacation is looking a lot better."

❑ "I couldn't be more content. Are you as relaxed as I am?"

Singles Tours

Singles tours are similar to singles vacations, but they include the sight-seeing or touring of interesting landmarks as their primary goal. This, then, is an ideal way to travel to exciting far-away places or historical landmarks and, at the same time, meet potential dates. A love of traveling will be the common denominator between you and the single prospects you meet. If you are single and love to sightsee, this is one avenue you should definitely explore.

Lines for Singles Tours

❑ "Did you enjoy history when you were in school? I figure that's why you're on this tour."

❑ "Have you traveled with any other tour groups?"

❑ "Forget the sightseeing! I'll just sit here and look at you!"

Singles Cruises

Singles cruises are yet another option for unattached people—one that many think is the most relaxing way to travel. Some singles cruises are just one-day outings. An example is an evening river cruise, where a large group of local singles meets to mingle under romantic moonlight. This type of singles cruise generally features food and dancing, along with a host of opportunities to meet prospects in a dressy evening atmosphere. It is very similar to a singles party or a singles luncheon or dinner, and you can use the steps and lines described on pages 62 to 66 to make contact with prospects.

However, there's another type of singles cruise. It is a vacation cruise, which is usually booked through a travel agent. The travel agent will work through a tour packager such as Single World, which organizes groups of singles and books them onto Norwegian, Carnival, or Royal Caribbean cruise ships. You can cruise to any number of lovely island paradises for up to two weeks. If desired, you can share a cabin (and the expense) with a roommate who has been matched to you according to gender, age, and smoking habits.

The food on a cruise is usually excellent, and the complete jam-packed schedule of activities is hard to believe. Singles who have taken cruises have found them to be wonderful vacations even if they don't produce a love connection. For more information, contact your local travel agent or Single World (1-800-223-6490).

Lines for Singles Cruises

❑ "One look at you and I don't think that I could ever be seasick."

❑ "How did you find out about this cruise?"

❑ "Are you on this cruise to look for other fish in the sea?"

❑ "Do you already have a plan or would you join me for _____?" *(Insert appropriate meal.)*

❑ "I don't know what I'd rather do—gaze at the stars above or gaze at you." *(This line is for use on clear evenings.)*

Adult Singles Camps

Adult singles camps are where single adults can go to enjoy a weekend, week, or more of sleep-away-camp fun and games. Many, if not most, of the camp activities are designed to bring singles together.

Adult singles camps are similar to singles cruises and singles weekend get-aways except for the atmosphere. Campers generally sleep in cots, eat in a mess hall, and wear jeans. You can meet other singles while hiking through the woods, roasting marshmallows over the campfire, participating in a craft workshop, playing a team sport, or joining in a myriad of other social events. Activities generally run from early in the morning until late in the evening and provide a wide range of choices to cater to most everyone's tastes.

The adult singles camp atmosphere is low-key and unpretentious, so you will likely meet down-to-earth prospects. If you liked camp as a child, chances are you'll love camp for single adults.

Lines for Singles Camps

❏ "Is my marshmallow supposed to catch on fire like this, or just get brown?"

❏ "I feel like Hansel and Gretel. Stay with me, and I'll protect you from the witch!" *(This line is for use during a hike in the woods.)*

❏ "I like the outfit you're wearing. It looks comfortable, functional—and sets off your eyes."

Singles Gambling Junkets

Singles gambling junkets are for singles who love to gamble. Sign up for a bus, train, or plane ride to Las Vegas, Reno, Atlantic City, or the many other casino resort areas for a day or weekend of gambling. Also on the outing will be other singles who love the action and the environment of a casino. You'll be able to meet prospects traveling to and back, while gambling, during dinner, or while participating in any other activity with your group.

Lines for Singles Gambling Junkets

❏ "One look at you, and I feel like I'm going to have good luck at the tables."

❏ "I'd love to have you right at my side for good luck."

❏ "Would you like to try your luck and join me for _____?" *(Insert appropriate meal.)*

Singles Retreats

Many people, including singles, go on retreats. Retreats offer quiet, contemplative, and therapeutic atmospheres away from the topsy-turvy real world. You may unexpectedly find the perfect companion while unwinding at a retreat. If you don't, you'll be well-rested and refreshed for meeting prospects when you return home.

Retreats are frequently sponsored by religious organizations, so you can inquire about them at your house of worship. You could also do an online search; type in the keyword "retreat," the religion or faith you follow and, perhaps, a general location.

Lines for Retreats

❏ "Isn't this quiet wonderful?"

❏ "Would you like to join me for a stroll in the garden/around the lake/in the woods?"

When a group of singles travel together, there is adventure to be had in every sense of the word. Each person starts the journey with optimism that a good time will be had and great prospects will be found. Singles travel opportunities bring together groups of people who crave excitement, culture, and learning. If that sounds like your kind of crowd, why not find out where the next voyage is heading?

CONCLUSION

This chapter has provided yet a few more ideas for those who have discovered that singles events and clubs are a viable, even creative way to meet prospects. As you continue reading Part II, you will find plenty of additional avenues, but the following chapters focus less on organized singles functions. They cover a broader spectrum of locations and activities geared toward bringing people of similar interests together to have fun. However, we make note of any sports and activities that do offer specific singles functions as well.

12

Personal Interests—
Professional
to Political

*H*ave you ever thought about just how many interests, hobbies, and passions you have? Moreover, have you ever asked yourself how each could lead you to new prospects? Start with your job. Are there professional functions that place you in the company of singles? Next, think about your leisure interests and hobbies. Do you like to practice martial arts, do crafts, meditate, or write poetry? So do many other singles! Why not join them? Call to mind your opinion on various causes and political agendas. Would you like to meet someone who has the same concerns?

Take the time to look at who you are—professionally and personally. Write down your interests and choose several of them to pursue. The more you get involved in groups and activities, the better your chances are of finding someone special. This chapter offers motivation and some ideas to get you started.

PROFESSIONAL ACTIVITIES

The workplace has always been a handy site for singles to meet because of the convenience factor. In a work environment, it is very natural for a relationship to develop and flourish. Many companies create opportunities for singles to meet and mingle with one another by organizing softball games. Different departments within the company play against each other. Some companies also belong to leagues, which pit local companies against one another and open up all sorts of horizons as far as prospects are concerned. Moreover, company parties at holiday time offer further opportunities for singles within the same firm to connect.

A major drawback of work-initiated personal relationships is that they sometimes affect the work relationship. An employer-employee relationship may bring about jealousy or charges of favoritism from coworkers. Also, if the personal relationship goes sour, so may the work relationship; uneasy feelings may be prevalent in one or both parties, which can make things awkward for everyone in the office. Jobs can sometimes even be jeopardized.

You should clearly evaluate the ramifications of a workplace romance before you allow yourself to become immersed in such a relationship. That being said, let's discuss some of the specific settings in which work can contribute to fun.

Industry Mixers, Workshops, And Seminars

Attending an industry mixer, workshop, or seminar is an excellent way to meet singles who work in your field. Industry mixers are held periodically to bring together people from all facets of the industry; many of these people are single. Often, wine and cheese parties are held to afford people a casual atmosphere for meeting, mingling, and developing new professional and personal relationships.

Industry workshops and seminars may also be offered to help you further develop your expertise and increase your knowledge in specific aspects of your industry. Workshops and seminars are often attended by sharp singles who are looking for career advancement and an increase in their net income.

If you are single and in a specific field, be sure to check your trade journals for the dates of industry mixers, workshops, and seminars. You will increase your skills, enlarge your network of professional acquaintances, and possibly meet an attractive prospect.

Lines for Industry Mixers, Workshops, and Seminars

❑ "What facet of this industry are you in?"

❑ "Are you planning on attending additional industry workshops/ seminars? Maybe we could go to one together."

❑ "Is this your first industry workshop/seminar?"

❑ "Are there any CDs available for this workshop/seminar?"

❑ "I'm planning on buying the corresponding tapes/CDs for this workshop/seminar. If you're not getting them, I'd be glad to make copies for you."

❏ "Will they be serving coffee and Danish during break? It's not an official break without coffee and Danish."

Trade Shows and Conventions

Attending or exhibiting at trade shows or conventions may be a part of your job. At conventions and trade shows, single people can be found selling their company's product or service, buying products or services for their company, or just furthering their product knowledge. Opportunities abound for singles with common interests to meet and connect.

Additionally, if you have an interest in any careers other than your own, you could attend a convention or trade show and possibly meet singles from totally unrelated fields. There are trade shows for just about every kind of business imaginable. You can find books and magazines at your local library that list the various trade shows and conventions for the entire year.

Lines for Conventions and Trade Shows

❏ "How long have you been in this line of work?"

❏ "I've been in this field for a few years now. How come I've never had the pleasure of meeting you before?"

❏ "How often do you attend these shows?"

Part-Time Jobs

If you are single and could use some extra money (and who couldn't?), try working a part-time job in a high traffic area with repeat customers, such as a gas station, restaurant, or convenience store. This type of work situation will put you in contact with a multitude of people, many of whom will be single. Also, a good choice would be a part-time job connected with one of your hobbies or areas of interest. For example, if you're a bicycling enthusiast, you could meet like-minded prospects through a part-time job at your local bicycle store.

Lines for Part-Time Jobs

❏ "What made you decide to take this job?"

❑ "Have you ever thought of working in this industry full-time?"

❑ "You are one of my favorite customers. I look forward to seeing you every week."

Hopefully, your professional life can do a little something for your personal life. Take full advantage of any work-related opportunities that will bring you into contact with new faces.

HOBBIES

Our culture is beginning to understand the health benefits of leisure activities. So most people have a few hobbies that allow them to take a break from the stress mode. But why spend time on these activities alone? Why not try to combine the pleasure you get from your favorite leisure activities with the chance to meet some interesting prospects? Below are a few examples of recreational hobbies that are not only good stress-relievers but good meeting grounds.

Arts and Crafts Fairs, Festivals, and Shows

Many people have an intense interest in arts and crafts, and there are many places where you can use this hobby to meet singles. For example, you could visit an arts and crafts fair, festival, or show, all of which feature a variety of artists and craftsmen displaying their wares. You'll find fine art, pottery, jewelry, leather goods, woodwork, baskets, fabrics, furniture, and blown glass. Events such as these are a great way to spend a day. Singles can be found selling wares, shopping, and browsing.

Similar to arts and crafts fairs, festivals, and shows are antique fairs, which are extremely popular in certain parts of the United States. Single antique buffs can enjoy meeting and mingling at these events.

Lines for Arts and Crafts Fairs, Festivals, and Shows

❑ "Would you like to join me as I window shop?"

❑ "What do you think of this as a birthday gift for my _____?" *(Insert "friend" or "relative.")*

❑ "I desperately need to get a last-minute gift for an artsy friend. You look like you've got good taste. Would you have any suggestions for me?"

Cat, Dog, and Horse Shows

There are many ways that pets can help you meet prospects. One unusual way is to go to a show featuring your favorite type of animal. There, you will find many animal lovers who appreciate the beauty of the animal kingdom.

For example, at a cat show, you'll find throngs of single feline fanciers. Cat shows bring all types of breeds under one roof. They also bring out cat-loving singles, as well as breeders and groomers who are single. Purr on over to an exciting prospect and discuss the benefits of being single and owning a cat. For example, cats make wonderful pets and require only a small amount of daily maintenance. Often, a single person's lifestyle does not provide the freedom to attend to a pet's needs, especially during the workday. However, a cat does not have to be walked every few hours. Add to that the beauty, gracefulness, and companionship that a cat provides, and you've got a winning pet for a single person! As you make these points and show your admiration of the animals, conversation will flow naturally.

Dogs are man's—and woman's—best friend, and people just love them. Some people love their dogs so much that they want to groom them and show them off at area dog shows. Dog shows display canines of all sizes, shapes, and breeds. They generally teem with single people raving over a variety of dogs. If you're a dog lover, or just an animal lover in general, dog shows are an ideal spot to meet attractive singles out for a fun time.

Single horse lovers should make it a point to attend horse shows. Attractive single prospects can usually be found either appreciating the horses or proudly displaying them. There's no law against looking at a beautiful horse and simultaneously eyeing its attractive single owner or groomer! Trot on over and make your move.

Lines for Cat, Dog, and Horse Shows

❏ "Do you have a cat/dog/horse at home?"

❏ "What's your favorite breed?"

❏ "I admit, I'm one of those obsessed cat owners who would do anything for his animal. How about you?"

❏ "I have a crazy dog. He has a fear of being bitten by our mailman."

❏ "You look so noble standing by that beautiful horse! You must have royal blood!"

❏ "If you're going to flash that blue ribbon smile at me, don't you think you ought to know my name?"

❏ "My cat/dog/horse would love you, and he's very selective."

Fan Clubs and Conventions

Is there a TV series or a rock group that you absolutely adore? Let's look at a television series, for example. *Star Trek* has spawned fan clubs and science fiction conventions around the country and the world. Fans of the show can join clubs to receive newsletters or "fanzines," memorabilia, and news of upcoming events such as autograph parties and conventions. The conventions are often held in huge auditoriums or arenas and draw thousands of the faithful. You don't need to be a member of a club to attend a convention, however. Conventions are open to the public, and they draw hundreds of the mildly interested and just curious, too.

If you're a Trekkie or a serious fan of another show, you should consider joining the fan club associated with your interest. The television show around which a club is formed might fade into boob-tube heaven someday, but maybe you'll have found someone to watch your old tapes with. Regular meetings are generally not part of fan club agendas, but local members may meet occasionally for lunch, cocktails, or even rerun marathons. Some clubs also feature pen pal services.

As briefly suggested above, television shows are not the only things that attract fans. Many musical performers have fan club followings, as do a number of actors, actresses, athletes, sports teams, and the like. As long as a person is not unhealthily obsessed with a celebrity personality, a band, or a sports team, you can enjoy sharing a passion and nurturing each other's interests.

Lines for Fan Clubs and Conventions

❏ "Do you know where the Gilligan's Island booth is? Only kidding." *(This line to be said with humor.)*

❏ "Who's your favorite character on this show?"

❏ "What do you think was the best _____ episode?" *(Insert name of show.)*

❏ "You won't believe this, but I just saw two people get beamed up in the restroom. Have you also noticed anything funny going on?" *(This line and the following two lines are for use at a science fiction convention.)*

❏ "I would like to thank the powers that be for beaming your molecules into my path." *(This is also for use at a science fiction convention.)*

❏ "Are we bonding or is this just an unexpectedly pleasant cosmic encounter?"

❏ "Do you know when _____'s next concert is? And would you like to go?" *(Insert name of star.)*

❏ "Do you think the rumors about _____ are true?" *(Insert the name of the star.)*

   — *(Reply)* "What rumors?"

   — "_____ wants us very much to meet."

Once you identify the hobbies that you enjoy—if you haven't found them already—do some research. Read through area publications, look at library bulletin boards, and search the internet for activities that are taking place around you. If you pursue a few hobbies, you are going to meet people who know how to enjoy themselves and who like to unwind in the same ways that you do.

SELF-HELP

Life tends to be fast-paced and stressful. So these days, many people are in pursuit of a healthier state of mental and physical awareness. Have you started any self-help activities for the body, mind, and spirit? If not, it's time to think about joining an exercise or meditation class, or even a support group that could help you find release. While you're improving your body, mind, and spirit, you could also be improving your love life!

Fitness Centers

Fitness centers offer you a wide range of activities. Most often, a general membership offers the use of many exercise machines; the privilege of attending aerobics, spinning, and step classes (just to name a few); access to a pool and, perhaps, sauna; and a counter at which to buy health shakes and salads. Along with these perks, you have a chance to meet other singles. So throw on some stylish fitness wear and get into shape.

Yet another benefit of fitness centers is that you often see prospects in their natural state. What you see is what you get, so there should be no surprises or disappointments later on. At one time, co-ed fitness centers, gyms, and workout clinics were a prime location for singles to meet and mingle, and the environment was more like a club than a health facility. People now, however, are more conscientious about getting and keeping themselves in shape, so they go to fitness centers for the primary purpose of working out. The atmosphere is no longer as contrived, yet fitness centers are still a viable location for connecting with other singles. Go ahead and stretch your boundaries!

Lines for Fitness Centers

❏ "I'm exhausted. Do you know CPR in case I collapse?"

❏ "Would you join me in an aerobic sprint to the juice bar for a drink?"

❏ "They pay you to work out here . . . am I right?"

❏ "Just looking at you has rejuvenated all the cells in my body. I want to thank you, and all of my cells thank you."

Yoga and Transcendental Meditation Classes

Another way to meet interesting singles is to attend yoga or transcendental meditation (TM) classes. Yoga and TM are techniques that promote the finding of peace and tranquility within yourself. They can be ideal for singles who feel tense and stressed-out. These modes of relaxation promote balance of body and mind, bringing you into harmony with nature and the world around you.

By exploring your inner self through yoga or TM, you have the potential to become a better person. That alone should aid you in attracting and meeting other quality singles. In addition, once again, you're meeting people at these classes who share an interest with you, which may make them more receptive to developing a friendship or even a relationship. It seems like you can't lose if you join a yoga or meditation group.

Lines for Yoga and Transcendental Meditation Classes

❏ "I need yoga/TM to calm my heart after gazing at you."

❏ "How did you first become interested in yoga/TM?"

❏ "My heart is in yoga/TM, but my legs are putting up a little fuss." *(This line is for use when getting into or out of a difficult yoga posture or long-held meditation posture.)*

Support Groups

If you are a member of a support group, you know how valuable the help and advice of such groups can be. Have you thought of looking at your support group as a source of prospects, too? At your support group meetings, you have people who share your particular problem, understand what you are going through, and can offer sound advice from personal experience. Making closer contact with a single member from your group will not only bring you additional support in times of stress but also companionship for more lighthearted moments.

If you are single, have any kind of problem, and do not belong to a support group, remember that there is emotional support available for you, along with a good opportunity to meet single prospects who find themselves in a comparable situation. Support groups are established for almost every type of problem, from weight disorders to shyness, to alcoholism, to debilitating diseases such as cancer, diabetes, heart disease, and arthritis. Support groups are also available for the relatives and friends of people with serious problems. One word of caution: If you are in the initial stages of recovering from a severe problem, or your prospect is still working on achieving a sound state of body and mind, it would be best to wait until both parties are stable enough and ready for a healthy dating relationship.

Lines for Support Groups

❏ "How long have you been a member of this group?"

❏ "Would you like to go for a cup of coffee after the meeting?"

❏ "Will you be here next week?"

❏ "I like your voice. It's really soothing."

❏ "You have a pretty smile. It really makes me feel good when I see you smile."

Single Parent Clubs

Single parent clubs offer an opportunity for single, divorced, or widowed parents to meet and connect with each other. These clubs are everywhere and include single parents of all ages. Many of these clubs are affiliated with a church or religious organization.

If you are a single parent, be sure to join a single parent club in your area. An example is Parents Without Partners. These clubs generally hold meetings on a regular basis, as well as sponsor mixers, outings, and other social events. In addition to meeting prospects, you can become friends with people of either sex who have similar family situations.

Lines for Single Parent Clubs

❏ "Where do your children go to school?"

❏ "Who is your child's pediatrician?"

❏ "How do you deal with your child when he talks back/throws a tantrum/misses curfew?"

There are so many levels to life, and it's hard to keep all of them functioning maximally. Why not help yourself out by joining a self-help activity? You are likely to meet singles who are experiencing the same stresses as you are and who enjoy being around people who can share in their challenges—and have a good time while doing so.

CHARITY INTERESTS AND POLITICAL CAUSES

What do you feel passionate about? There are many organizations that are looking for volunteers, and you can both help an organization that you support and enhance your efforts to meet singles. If you have a favorite charity or civic group, find out how you can get involved with it. If you're not sure what group you'd like to join, speak to other people. Check under "Organizations," "Charities," or "Associations" (among other headings) in the Yellow Pages, or ask your local librarian for suggestions. You can even do a keyword search on the internet; type the name of the cause that interests you and your location, and see what pops up. Let's discuss some examples in this category.

Charitable Groups

A fine way to meet singles is to join a charitable group. You will enjoy being around people who share a strong interest with you and who are selfless enough to give of themselves generously. A success story in this category involves an independent twenty-four-year-old single woman named Shawn. Here's her story:

"One committee that I'm on is a branch of the American Heart Association. Every year, my county's chapter has a bachelor auction fund raiser. This is the second year in a row that I'll be in the Bachelor Recruiting Department. What a great way to meet single men! I've dated a couple of the guys here and there. Nothing serious, but a good time.

"Recently, for this year's auction, some people at work told me to recruit their friend. He is thirty years old, good looking, and owns a dry cleaner here in town. I called him, introduced myself, and told him why I was calling. I stopped by his store one night to give him details about the bachelor auction. He was receptive to the whole idea. I told him I'd get back to him for the interview we'd have to do.

"Needless to say, I have disqualified him from the auction. For the past month, we've been an item, and at this point, neither one of us is interested in having him in the auction! Maybe I have never met anyone in a supermarket or library, but silly me, I was definitely taking my clothes to the wrong dry cleaner! I've been working less than a mile away from him for two years.

"A lot of 'finding the right people' is being involved in committees like I am. I strongly suggest this for single women. Plus, you are doing things for the community and society. You use your time wisely (not in bars), and you feel good because you do something worthwhile."

There are other ways you can get involved with charitable groups. You can join volunteer committees that work to raise funds, increase public awareness, or enlist support for organizations such as the Arthritis Foundation, Leukemia Society, AIDS Foundation, Lupus Foundation, and American Cancer Society. Other charitable groups aid the homeless, help underprivileged children, or fight world hunger. Volunteering your time will not only help your chosen organization in its efforts but can put you in touch with other singles who have similar concerns and values. Furthermore, as a "do gooder," you will generate positive energy, which will help you to attract quality prospects.

Singles are out there, and there's a good chance that you'll meet the right prospect if you get involved with a charitable group. And even if there are no other singles on your volunteer committee, you may be able to network yourself into meeting an eligible prospect through a new-found committee friend.

Lines for Charitable Groups

❑ "I can't believe you're interested in this cause too! It's so important to me."

❑ "I am going to file an official protest if I don't find an open seat next to you at our next meeting."

❑ "Did you see today's newspaper?" *(This line is for use when an article of interest to your charitable group was included in the newspaper.)*

Environmental Groups

Many people are sincerely concerned, and even outraged, over what the human race has done to the environment. They join environmental groups which try to prevent or repair the damages of air pollution, acid rain, nuclear radiation, ocean dumping, littering, and so on.

Singles who join causes such as these care enough about the world to lobby as a group for a safer environment, or to stand up and be heard individually at local meetings and public rallies. Chances are that the prospects you would meet fighting for the environment would be persons with the right kind of values.

Lines for Environmental Groups

❑ "What got you interested in this organization?"

❑ "Weren't you at the rally downtown/at City Hall/in Washington last year?"

❑ "The environment is a great reason to meet you . . . though any reason would be a great reason to meet *you*."

Animal Rights Groups

Are you outraged at the widespread cruelty of animals at the hands of various industries? Many singles get involved with animal rights groups, along with the related meetings, rallies, protests, and marches. If you are a single animal lover, you will meet other concerned singles who believe in the humane treatment of all animals.

Associations in this category include People for the Ethical Treatment of Animals (PETA), Friends of Animals, the Humane Society, the ASPCA, the American Antivivisection Association, and the Doris Day Animal Welfare League, just to name a few. All of these groups provide situations where animal-loving singles can meet, mingle, and bond.

Lines for Animal Rights Groups

❏ "How long have you been working with this organization?"

❏ "I am really glad I came tonight. I love animals so much, and I feel I can actually do some good with this group."

❏ "Do you have any pets at home?"

Community Groups

Savvy singles know the value of a safe and fun locale. They are community-oriented and enjoy being involved in their neighborhoods or towns. Therefore, an excellent way to meet geographically desirable singles is to join a community group. You can either get involved in the planning end of community events or just be a participant.

Examples of common local events are bazaars, parades, fairs, festivals, auctions, block parties, and celebrations for holidays such as the Fourth of July, Thanksgiving, New Year's Day, and Labor Day. Keep abreast of local events. Note dates and locations on your calendar. You undoubtedly will meet some singles.

Lines for Community Groups

❏ "I can't think of anyone I'd rather have in my group."

❏ "This committee needs rounding out—you could supply the beauty/brains/humor."

❏ "I love this town, and I'm really enjoying doing something valuable for it."

❏ "I recently moved here. Do you know a good place to meet singles?"

❏ "It's great to meet someone nice from this area. I also was born, bred, and buttered here."

Political Groups and Committees

Another fine way to meet singles is to join a political group or committee. Political affiliations, such as the Republican and Democratic parties, have meetings, rallies, voter registration drives, cocktail parties, and the like, where many politically oriented singles can be found. You can also join a political campaign, where you can work with other singles for the election of a specific candidate.

If you are single and like politics, be sure to get involved in a political group or committee. You'll increase your odds of meeting prospects with parallel political interests. You greatly increase your chances of meeting intelligent, passionate individuals. Also, make it a priority to vote during all major and local elections. After you've voted, stick around the polling station to meet attractive prospects. You can discuss the election, and politics in general, with anyone you find interesting.

Lines for Political Groups and Committees

❏ "I'm glad that you're on our team."

❏ "I want to be a member of whatever political party you're affiliated with."

❏ "I'd like to nominate you for President/State Senator/County Commissioner."

❏ "Can you tell me where the radicals are meeting?"

Fellow politics lovers want to hear from you. Those who are interested in politics love the debates, hot issues, and the passions that abound in the political environment. You will meet many exciting, intelligent, and motivated people at political group meetings and campaigns.

EDUCATION AND INTELLECT

There's nothing like a good education to enhance one's life. And there's nothing like an educational setting for meeting singles. Perhaps you have a couple of classes left before you can get your degree. Maybe you'd enjoy taking adult education courses, or attending lectures on subjects that interest you. In any of these situations, you are going to meet singles who possess that wonderful spark of intellectual curiosity.

College and Adult Education Courses and Workshops

Besides pursuing an advanced degree, many single people attend college or adult education courses and workshops to meet other singles with similar interests. Sing up for a course in writing, history, or art at your community college. Research the fine arts classes at local art leagues and schools—painting, sculpting, photography. If none of those work for you, how about jewelry-making or cooking? The possibilities are endless. You'll be amazed at how many singles are searching for someone to share their intellectual and artistic interests with.

Workshops are also popular with singles. You can take workshops on subjects such as developing relationships, building self-esteem, gaining financial independence, and selling real estate. Workshops tend to demand less of a commitment because they are either one-day programs or meet just a few times.

Lines for College and Adult Education Courses and Workshops

❏ "What made you decide to take this course/workshop?"

❏ "How long have you been interested in this subject?"

❏ "If you need a study partner, I'd certainly be willing to volunteer."

❏ "Do you mind if I look at your notes?"

Lectures

Lectures, either in a college setting or in other places, are another ideal way to meet single prospects. Lectures on a variety of subjects are publicized in college and local newspapers, on radio, and on television. Also look for flyers in your local library or at your favorite bookstore. A lecture on a particular book, a specific time in history, or a scientific phenomenon might be the very environment that connects you with a wonderful prospect.

When attending a lecture, be sure to keep your eyes open for attractive singles. Make eye contact with those around you, dress well, and smile a lot. During a break in the lecture, during the question and answer session, or at refreshment time, strike up a conversation with a prospect. Prospects might be attending the lecture or they might be working at the hall.

Remember that you can attend college lectures even if you've been out of college for years or never went to college. But do have a genuine interest in the subject being discussed, so that you will sound somewhat knowledgeable when you strike up a conversation with an exciting prospect.

Lines for Lectures

❑ "How long have you been interested in this subject?"

❑ "Have you done any other reading/research/studying on this subject?"

❑ "What did you think of this lecture/lecturer?"

❑ "Have you ever been to the museum? It has an incredible collection of related items, memorabilia, and information on this subject."

School Meetings and Events

If you are a single parent—and the world is full of them—try to attend as many Parent-Teacher Association (PTA) meetings as possible at your child's school. Besides receiving important information about the school, its curriculum, and its problems, you will also meet and interact with many other single parents, as well as single teachers. One of those single parents or teachers might be very happy that you decided to attend that meeting. If you are interested in being involved with the larger community, consider school board meetings.

In addition to PTA and school board meetings, many other events are staples in the school calendar. Is your child in a play? In the orchestra or band? On the football team? How many children in these groups have single parents watching them perform? Also leave room in your schedule for the carnivals, learning fairs, and other events that your child might either be participating in or would just like to attend in your company.

If you don't have a child of your own, try to "borrow" one. Is your sister or brother too busy to take your niece or nephew to the May Day Fair? Is your neighbor's child helping out at the Fifth Grade Car Wash?

Use your imagination. As many parents are quick to point out, when you have children, your circle of friends enlarges one-hundred-fold.

Lines for School Meetings and Events

❏ "Who are your child's teachers?"

❏ "Do you ever wish you were back in school again?"

❏ "Do your children get a lot of homework?"

❏ "I can't believe how much these desks have shrunk!"

❏ "Did you go to _____? You look very familiar." *(Insert name of school.)*

If you love being in an intellectual environment and sharing good conversation, register for a course or sign up for a lecture. Even attend school board or PTA meetings. By doing so, you will certainly enrich your mind. In the long run, you will be a better listener and conversationalist because you have exercised your intellectual muscles. But you also will quite possibly enrich your personal life.

CONCLUSION

Clearly, whether you are at work or at play, you can use your greatest passions to lead you to like-minded singles. Once you choose a few of your favorite interests and put forth the energy to nurture activities related to those interests, you are bound to meet great people who are easy to talk with and fun to be around.

13

Sports and Outdoor Recreation—Ballgames to the Beach

There is an ever-increasing need for creative ways to bring singles together. Since many single people have at least a marginal interest in sports, while others are sports fanatics, it stands to reason that sports outings and leagues are an ideal way to meet interesting prospects. In addition, many singles are into fitness, health, athletics, and the great outdoors. So outdoor activities are natural forums for similar-minded singles to meet.

SPORTS

We could write a whole book on the various sports venues that are conducive to matchmaking. But we chose a couple of the most widely available, affordable, and popular sports activities for this chapter. Once you start reading through the following sections on competitive sports teams and sports opportunities, you're likely to come up with a few of your own ideas. Write them down and pursue further information from your local phone book, newspapers, YMCAs, health clubs, and the like.

Softball

Softball games are primarily held in warm weather and bring out a good crowd. Men generally like playing on softball teams, and women looking to meet single men will find plenty of them here. Many games are played at local parks and fields. Some teams are comprised of coworkers or those in the same profession; others are groups of lifetime friends and local buddies. Then there are teams, some of which are coed, that are open to local residents. Perhaps you can sign up with a team and widen your social circle. Even if you are a heterosexual playing on a single-sex team, you can at least start networking. (See Chapter 3.)

Also, consider being a spectator—maybe you can convince a couple of friends to come along. Frequent the same parks and fields; let your face be known. Cheer enthusiastically—but don't overdo it. Sooner or later, you're likely to start talking to an athletic prospect.

Lines for Softball

❏ "We play great together. You and I should start our own league."

❏ "You can use my glove/bat. I only lend it to special people."

❏ "You look great out there in the field. You're a natural."

❏ "It wouldn't be a softball game without you here."

❏ "I can't help but admire your speed and grace as a base runner."

Volleyball and Walleyball

Volleyball and walleyball games are wonderful for meeting prospects. The main difference between the two games is that you play walleyball in an enclosed racquetball court and can bounce the ball off any of the walls within the court. In both sports, your position on the playing court rotates due to the frequent change of servers. This creates many opportunities for you to meet prospects on both your team and the opposing team. Since both games require a team effort, a lot of new friendships and relationships can develop. Also, in subsequent games with different teams, as well as in-between games, many opportunities exist to make new connections. Consider joining volleyball and walleyball leagues, too, which will help bring you in touch with other singles who enjoy these sports.

Lines for Volleyball and Walleyball

❏ "I may not know you, but I want you on my team."

❏ "I definitely want you on all my volleyball/walleyball teams."

❏ "How long have you been playing volleyball/walleyball?"

❏ "You give our volleyball/walleyball team a good look."

❏ "You have a great kill shot."

❏ "Can I buy you a drink after our game?"

Bowling

If you like to bowl, another way to meet prospects is to attend singles bowling outings or to join a singles bowling league. Singles bowling outings are one-time events designed to bring singles together. Even if you've never bowled or aren't particularly thrilled with the sport, it's still worthwhile to attend one of these outings. Many singles show up, more because they are interested in finding someone special than they are in impressing others with their bowling skills. If you're a decent bowler, it's a plus, but it's not necessary for a singles bowling outing.

The same is true for singles bowling leagues. The only difference is that singles bowling leagues are for singles who truly enjoy bowling, since leagues play regularly, on a specific day every week. It doesn't matter what your skill level is, just as long as you enjoy bowling.

There's always the option of attending bowling events that are not specifically geared toward singles as well, and simply frequenting your local bowling alley. You are bound to meet friendly bowlers who, if not single themselves, might eventually be able to set you up with someone who shares your interest in the sport.

Lines for Bowling

❏ "How long have you been bowling?"

❏ "What's your bowling average?"

❏ "I would gladly polish your bowling ball or buff your shoes."

❏ "You may not knock down a lot of pins, but you've sure bowled me over."

Tennis

Tennis is a sport that is enjoyed with equal interest by women and men, so there are often large turnouts for tennis outings. Singles tennis outings are specifically for singles who enjoy the game of tennis. Get your tennis racquet out of the closet, throw on some sporty tennis wear, and sign up for singles tennis. You may be surprised to learn that you can love tennis and fall in love with a tennis-loving prospect both at the same time.

Many parks have tennis courts for public use. If you like tennis and want to meet other tennis-lovers without going on specific singles outings, just visit your local public tennis courts often. Convince a friend to go with you so that you can get on the court and play. After using the courts a few times, you'll probably start to see the same faces. Strike up a conversation with the other players or spectators when you feel comfortable. There's a good chance that some of them will be single or know single people who love the sport. You can always begin a conversation by asking for some tips on the game.

Lines for Tennis

❏ "How long have you been playing tennis?"

❏ "What type of racquet do you prefer—regular or oversized?"

❏ "You have a great tennis style. If I take you out to dinner, would you give me some lessons?"

❏ "Would you be interested in being my doubles partner?"

❏ "What type of court surface do you prefer?"

❏ "What type of sneakers do you find are best for playing tennis?"

❏ "Have you ever played on a _____ court?" *(Insert type of surface.)*

Skiing

Skiing has always been a popular sport among single people. Therefore, singles ski weekends tend to draw a wonderful crowd of single ski buffs. If you don't like formal singles gatherings, go to a popular resort with a fun group of friends. Ski resorts have booming social scenes. Many single people are bound to be there with *their* friends and your initial contact will seem very natural.

Skiing is an excellent sport and requires quite a bit of athleticism. For this reason, you will probably meet athletic, well-conditioned prospects. You can find prospects on the ski lift, on the slopes, in front of the lodge fireplace sipping hot chocolate, and even in the infirmary!

Don't overlook the fact that you can also join a ski club. There, you can regularly meet singles who share your interest in the sport.

Lines for Skiing

❏ "For how long have you been skiing?"

❏ "Can I get you a cup of hot _____?" *(Insert beverage.)*

❏ "Consider me your personal ski slope attendant if you wipe out anywhere near me."

❏ "Would you believe that I planned this injury just to meet you?" *(This line is for use in the infirmary.)*

❏ "Do you know any good local places to eat/go dancing?"

❏ "I'm looking forward to seeing you on the slopes. Actually, I'm looking forward to seeing you anywhere."

Golf

Golf is one of Americans' favorite games. It's also a favorite game of singles for two good reasons—it's easy to be placed in a foursome with other singles, and once you are thrown together with new people, you have plenty of time to get to know them. Check with your local golf courses to find out how they pair their golfers and if they have special "tee-off" times for singles. Then grab your clubs and start swinging!

If you are a duffer with relatively little experience, there's nothing wrong with signing up for golf lessons, either at the golf course or in an adult education setting. You may find that there are other singles with the same idea, and you may start meeting prospects even before you get out on the links!

Lines for Golf

❏ "How long have you been playing golf?"

❏ "What's your handicap?"

❏ "Where did you learn to play golf like that?"

❏ "There's nothing like the game of golf to get you to enjoy the outdoors."

❏ "I used to get really teed off. Now all I do is tee off!"

Horseback Riding

Whether you own a horse or are just a horseback riding enthusiast, another way to meet single prospects is to join a horseback riding club. Horseback riding clubs offer members an opportunity to share the thrills and joys of horseback riding while on fascinating excursions. Rides are planned for all times of the day, so just about any schedule can be met. Single prospects can be found as club members, trainers, groomers, horse owners, stable investors, or staff members, all of whom have that one strong love of horses as the common bond.

One way to meet other single prospects through a horseback riding club is to get to the stable about fifteen to thirty minutes before the scheduled time and mingle with the other members. If you find a prospect you're interested in, you can canter together during the ride.

To join a horseback riding club, contact local stables and academies, which are listed in the Yellow Pages. Look in the sports section of your local newspaper for a listing of horse shows and the names of the stables, academies, or clubs sponsoring them. Horse or equestrian magazines, found in bookstores and on newsstands, may also provide some leads.

Lines for Horseback Riding Clubs

❏ "How long have you been horseback riding?"

❏ "That's a beautiful horse. What's his name?"

❏ "That horse has a very pleasant disposition. Did you just feed him? That's the way I am, too—feed me and I suddenly become pleasant."

If you are good at playing sports—even if you're not good at sports but enjoy playing a game anyway—why not make the most out of an already good time. Join a team or sign up for a few games. You just might score!

SPORTING EVENTS

If you are a sports fan, then going out to a live sporting event to root for your local team is an excellent way to meet prospects. Cheering for the home team or just showing an interest in a particular sport can be enough to get a relationship going. So get some friends or family together, purchase a bunch of tickets, and have a great time screaming from the stands. Don't forget to buy a momento—a T-shirt or baseball hat—with the name of your team on it, for use as an attention-grabber or conversation piece when you are elsewhere.

Lines for Sporting Events

❏ "How long have you rooted for this team?"

❏ "Do you come to many games?"

❏ "Would you be interested in joining our tailgating party?"

❏ "I'm sorry I'm cheering so loudly, but I get so excited about these players. Are you a diehard fan too?"

SPORTS BARS

Single people who enjoy nightlife should check out the fast-growing crop of sports bars in their local area. Sports bars are usually colorful watering holes that feature walls adorned with sports memorabilia, giant-screen televisions, lots of video and electronic sports games, and sports-themed dance floors. Conversation is easy because there are so many interesting things to comment on and countless things to do with prospects. Sports bars are terrific sites for meeting other singles and having fun at the same time.

Lines for Sports Bars

❏ "Would you like to share a snack while we watch our team devour the opponents?"

❏ "Our team can't lose with you rooting for them."

❏ "Would you join me for a halftime dance?"

❏ "Let's toast our team."

OUTDOOR ACTIVITIES

Meeting new people can be like inhaling a breath of fresh air. And what better place to get that breath of fresh air than in the great outdoors? If you like to commune with nature and want to share your experiences with new friends, consider the many different outdoor activities that are available for your enjoyment.

Beaches And Pools

Beaches and pools have always been known as great places for meeting other singles. Beaches are mainly a summertime meeting place, unless you're in a southern clime, so you have to make the most of them during the proper season. Of course, not all parts of the country have beaches, but more and more resort areas are building their own—even without oceans!

Slip into your most happening swimwear and make something happen. Pick a prime location and set up camp. Bring out all your gear—beach blanket, Frisbee, sunblock, suntan lotion, cooler, radio, book, magazines—whatever it takes to get yourself comfortable. Then pick out some prospects and make your move. If the response you get is not to your liking, go for a walk along the beach. You'll find hordes of singles sunbathing, reading books or magazines, playing Frisbee or paddleball, walking, swimming, eating, or drinking, and each and every one will be a potential prospect.

And while we're thinking about the water, pools are another good idea. Town pools, and even pools at local hotels, can be great sites for singles. Of course, there are indoor pools as well, for those who live in areas with rainy and snowy months.

Lines for Beaches and Pools

❏ "Can I get you a towel/drink/some munchies?"

❏ "Can I pull up a lounge chair/blanket next to you?"

❏ "I feel like enjoying this amazing sunset. Will you join me for a walk on the beach?"

❏ "May I double-park on your sand for a while?"

❏ "My sundial led me in your direction."

❏ "Have there been any attacks on swimmers/surfers by sharks or crazed tuna?"

❏ "You have the best-looking swimsuit at the pool/on the beach."

❏ "Do you know why some suntan lotions/sunblocks are proud that they have PABA while others advertise that they're PABA-free?"

❏ "How often should you reapply suntan lotion/sunblock on an average day at the beach?"

❏ "Could you please tell me the secret of applying suntan lotion/ sunblock without gluing sand to my entire body?"

❏ "Could you spare some ice for my water bottle?" *(This line is for use with a prospect who has a cooler.)*

❏ "I was ready to split, but seeing you makes me want to stay. What's your name?"

Parks

Whether they're in the country or the city, parks have a pleasant, restful, stress-free atmosphere. Take a walk in your local park and you're apt to encounter singles relaxing on benches, walking dogs, reading books or magazines, lounging on the grass, sunbathing, or taking a lunch break. Around lunchtime, parks usually draw a good crowd of single people.

Scan the park for prospects and pick out the best location for making contact with the most appealing. Or, park yourself on a bench that is in the direct path of prospects who are walking or bicycling. Perhaps you will be "discovered" by an attractive prospect because you were in the right location to be seen. You can also walk your dog, if you have one, since dogs are phenomenal conversation starters.

It's always a good idea to bring along a book. If you're "reading," any contact you make will seem accidental or natural, as opposed to contrived. You'll look as though you came to the park to read and relax, when in actuality, you cleverly were there to go prospecting!

Lines for Parks

❏ "Is this a beautiful day or what?"

❏ "I've heard that book is good. How do you like it so far?"

❏ "Will you join me for a walk in the park?"

❏ "I'm the best mosquito repellant around!"

❏ "I hope the rest of my day looks as good as you do." *(This line is for use in the morning or at lunchtime.)*

❏ "It's so nice to see a beautiful woman/handsome man like you on such a beautiful day."

Camping

Campers are serious nature lovers. If you like to camp, you should be with someone who can enjoy this outdoor activity with you. How do you meet such a someone? Singles camping trips are a great way to meet prospects who are outdoorsy and nature-loving. But you've got to like sleeping in tents and be pretty much oblivious to bugs.

There are lots of single prospects who love "roughing it," especially if there are perks—toasted marshmallows, hot chocolate, ghost stories in the dark. Make yourself available for the next singles camping excursion and nuzzle up to your favorite prospect beside a toasty campfire.

Lines for Singles Camping Trips

❏ "Would you allow me to be your guide through camp?"

❏ "Would you join me in the mess hall for _____?" *(Insert appropriate meal.)*

❏ "You're just the type of person I like to roast marshmallows with."

❏ "I need a partner to help set up the tent, prepare the food, etc. Do you want to be my camping buddy?"

Hay Rides

A hay ride is a classic way to meet fun-loving prospects—especially if it's a singles hay ride. People have been going on hay rides and meeting this way for years. The informal nature of a hay ride lends itself to a casual atmosphere where conversation is easy. Hay rides are festive and fun.

A new type of hay ride is the "haunted hay ride," during which riders are driven through a farm, field, or forest area where scary creatures are supposedly prowling. Of course, you'll want to get close to, and snuggle up with, someone you like. Hence, haunted hay rides can be effective at bringing singles together.

Lines for Singles Hay Rides

❏ "Have you ever been on a hay ride before?"

❏ "I can't think of anyone I'd rather be on a hay ride with than you."

❏ "Hey! Do you think we can smoke this stuff?" *(This line should be said with obvious humor.)*

❏ "I used to belong to Hay Riders Anonymous, but I just kept falling off the wagon!"

Bicycling

Bicycling is an incredible way to meet interesting singles. Besides being fun, it's ideal for promoting optimum health and an increased life span.

Singles interested in bicycling and in meeting other single cyclists can join bicycling clubs or participate in cycling tours or bike-a-thons. Bicycling clubs offer cyclists an opportunity to socialize at club meetings and on bicycling excursions to scenic and fascinating places. Bicycling tours are generally open to the public and are sponsored by bicycling clubs as a way to enlist new club members. Bike-a-thons are often sponsored by charities to help raise money.

While many singles bicycle for personal health and enjoyment, many others also pedal to prospect, which is exactly what you should do if you're single and love bicycling. Look for attractive prospects at bicycle club meetings, at the starting and finishing lines of sponsored events, while bicycling, and at rest stops and check points.

Lines for Bicycling Clubs, Bicycling Tours, and Bike-A-Thons

❑ "Would you mind if I ride along with you?"

❑ "This is a really nice area. Have you ever biked here before?"

❑ "Can I buy you some juice at the next rest stop?"

❑ "I love your bandage. Is it Ralph Lauren or Armani?" *(This line is for use with a bicyclist sporting a bandage.)*

❑ "I can't think of anyone I'd rather have blocking my wind."

❑ "Are your buns hurting as much as mine from this bicycle ride?"

Walking

Walking is another wonderful form of exercise. It's excellent for singles who want a good cardiovascular workout with a limited risk of injury. Any time you go for a walk, you have a chance to meet other people. Just keep your eyes open and be ready and willing to strike up a conversation with passersby.

The opportunity to meet other singles who enjoy walking or PowerWalking (a brisk form of walking) can be found by joining a walking club or attending a walkfest or walk-a-thon. Walkfests and walk-a-thons are usually sponsored by charities such as the American Diabetes Association, Multiple Sclerosis Society, and American Heart Association. They are usually held to raise money for research, in addition to offering people, many of whom are single, a fun day of walking for fitness.

Think about volunteering to work at a walkfest or walk-a-thon. You could help at the registration table or at a rest stop, where attractive single walkers may ask you for assistance.

Serious walkers can take this activity one step further by joining walking clubs. Club meetings provide dates and times of local planned walks, organize walking excursions, provide information on types of walking shoes, and the like. So, if you're interested in walking, a walking club is a great way to enjoy a hobby as well as possibly meet a love interest. Just stroll on over and make your move.

Lines for Walking Clubs, Walkfests, and Walk-A-Thons

❏ "Do you mind if I walk along with you?"

❏ "Nice walking shoes. What brand are they?"

❏ "Watch out for that pothole/cracked pavement/dog poop!"

❏ "Where did you learn to walk like that? You have some great moves.

❏ "Your feet must be really tired. You've been running/walking through my mind all day."

Skydiving and Mountain Climbing

For those singles who are truly adventurous, there are activities such as skydiving and mountain climbing. There are even clubs you can join to meet singles with these similar interests. If you like to walk the fine line, take some skydiving and mountain climbing lessons or join a club that arranges events for these sports. You might meet a single who sends you soaring!

Lines for Skydiving and Mountain Climbing

❏ "It takes a lot of courage to do this sport, but it's taking me even more courage to introduce myself. I'm _____."

❏ "I don't know whether I'm on an adrenaline high from that dive/climb or from being near you."

❑ "I've never dived in this area/climbed this mountain before. Have you?"

❑ "I'm getting those butterflies in my stomach. Any words of advice?"

The great outdoors are such a wonderful gift to us. Why not share your appreciation of that gift with someone special? By meeting prospects during outdoor activities, you can count on the fact that your new love interests will be willing to take in the fresh air, the sun, even the rain, with the same zest for life as you do.

CONCLUSION

If you are a sports fan or outdoor adventurer, you definitely should date someone who can appreciate your favorite mode of recreation. Take the time to do a little research and find a team, event, or location at which you can truly enjoy yourself. If you are having fun, people will want to be near you, talk to you, and join you. And while you're staying fit, you just might find the perfect "fit" for you!

14

Entertainment— Movies, Museums, and Music

here are many modes of entertainment that provide good meeting ground for singles. This chapter covers just a few of the most popular leisure events—cinema, music, and dance. These avenues of entertainment also offer pleasant social scenes where people are ready to relax and enjoy.

Most likely, there are all sorts of entertainment events that occur in the areas surrounding where you live or vacation. Hopefully, this chapter will inspire you to get out there and make the most of your evenings. By brushing up on your conversation skills, dressing well, and making yourself seen, you are likely to meet singles who share your appreciation of a good time.

MOVIE THEATERS

Movie theaters are really good places to find single prospects. Single people often get together with friends or go by themselves to see a movie. Look for prospects standing on the ticket line, waiting at the concession stand, milling in the lobby before or after the movie, sitting in the theater before the movie starts, or exiting the building.

Movies are popular for dates. For this reason, it is best to approach only those prospects you are sure are out with friends or by themselves! If you work it right, you might see a terrific film and also meet an equally terrific prospect.

Lines for Movie Theaters

❏ "What movie are you going to see?" *(This line should be used only in multiplex theaters; otherwise, you'll sound pretty foolish!)*

❏ "Have you heard any reviews about this movie?"

❏ "All of a sudden, I wish I was seeing whatever movie you're going to be seeing."

❏ "I hate waiting on ticket lines. I'm a terrible waiter."

❏ "I just come here for the trailers. How about you?"

❏ "I'll buy the popcorn if you buy the drinks."

❏ "If your movie is sold out, what will you see instead?"

MUSEUMS AND ART GALLERIES

Museums and art galleries can be fascinating places to meet prospects. Take some positive action and get out to one of these cultural centers. Make yourself presentable, put on your glasses, and prepare to be culturally enriched.

When you go to a museum or gallery, don't be intimidated by the surroundings. The atmosphere is quiet and reserved, but this is because most of the visitors are concentrating on the exhibits. Communication is by no means prohibited; you can, and should, talk to other people—especially singles. For example, while sauntering through the museum or gallery, let's say you notice a very attractive person admiring a piece of art. As you admire this attractive person, you can sidle up next to her and make a clever statement. Speak about how fine art stands up to the test of time and that you've been depressed ever since your pet turtle destroyed your Andy Warhol rendition of Arnold Stang. It was the only piece of fine art in your collection that you really cherished.

All types of art museums, as well as museums of sports memorabilia, rock and roll, classic cars, wildlife, and other themes, are ideal places to meet interesting singles. You can find singles admiring the exhibits, paying admission, checking the directory, or even standing in the lobby.

Lines for Museums and Art Galleries

❏ "Have you ever seen anything more beautiful?"

❏ "I see you're admiring this unusual painting. What do you think of it?"

❏ "Have you seen any other work by this artist?"

❏ "I find it amazing that anyone could produce something like this. I'm all thumbs myself."

DANCE CLUBS

Dance clubs, of course, will always draw throngs of singles for the purposes of dancing, drinking, and meeting someone new. There's usually loud music, a vibrant atmosphere, and good food and drink. If you feel like being social and letting loose, this is your scene.

Country music, which is currently enjoying a popularity craze, has become a big draw for singles. For this reason, country music clubs are springing up all over the place. If you're looking to find prospects who also enjoy country music, or you just want to get out, kick up your heels, and have a grand old time, visit a country music club—or any type of music club—and enjoy yourself.

It's not surprising, though, that many singles do not care for the heavy crowds, the smoke-filled rooms, and the somewhat superficial nature of many dance clubs. Do not feel like a bore if this particular singles scene does not appeal to you. However, you could always give yourself a little push and try a club that has been recommended. You *could* meet someone at one of these clubs. And you could always use this setting as a place to practice your lines!

Lines for Dance Clubs

❏ "Would you like to dance?"

❏ "Do you think the music is loud enough?" (*This line works well when the music is deafeningly loud and you say it directly into your prospect's ear. It usually produces a laugh and breaks the ice.*)

❏ "Can I get you a drink?"

❏ "Would you like to get out of here and get some fresh air?"

SQUARE DANCES

Square dances can be lots of fun and are often loaded with singles. If you want to meet an attractive single prospect, this is a great place to do-se-do with a partner.

Learning to square dance is relatively easy, so most people—even those with two left feet—can pick up the basic steps within minutes.

Since you'll be swinging from partner to partner when you square dance, be sure to focus on the dancers you want to meet. You can also mosey on over and strike up a conversation on the sidelines while your initial prospect is resting.

Lines for Square Dances

❏ "I love the way you square dance."

❏ "You have some great square-dancing moves."

❏ "You must be square dancing for years. You do it so effortlessly."

❏ "I don't know you, but can I choose you to be my square-dancing partner?"

❏ "I feel so square, having not square danced with you yet."

❏ "I'd love to square dance this one with you."

❏ "Would you join me for a good square meal after this square dance?"

❏ "You're the one person I've been wanting to dance/speak with all night."

MUSIC FESTIVALS AND CONCERTS

A great place to meet singles is at a music festival or concert. Music festivals and concerts frequently offer an open-air atmosphere, with live musical groups, dancing, related merchandise, and refreshments. Besides working there, singles can be found attending the show or participating in any number of activities, so keep your eyes open for appealing prospects.

Whether you like country, rock and roll, rap, jazz, classical, folk, or any other type of music, you'll find music-related outings teeming with singles being moved by the sounds of their favorite recording artists. Since music generally has a positive effect on the spirit, mind, and physical being, chances are that the prospects you approach will be happy and receptive to you, especially because you're sharing their musical interest. Also, listening to your favorite music can help you feel good all over and will add to the positive energy you'll exude when you approach prospects in these surroundings. Finding someone special who appreciates the wonderful feelings that come from music can truly add to your life.

Lines for Music Festivals and Concerts

❏ "Do you have any of their cassettes or CDs?"

❏ "What's your favorite song/album by this band?"

❏ "Have you been to any other music festivals/concerts?"

❏ "I'm not sure if I'm smiling because I love the music or because I'm enjoying looking at you."

❏ "Would you join me in sharing some positive musical vibes?"

❏ "The best part of this festival/concert has been meeting you."

❏ "Can I buy you a Coke/Perrier/hot dog/slice of quiche/T-shirt?"

❏ "This music is giving me an out-of-body experience."

JAZZ CLUBS

Jazz music has always been known as the music of choice for ultra-hip, super-cool people. Now that mainstream society has come to accept jazz, singles everywhere are taking to jazz clubs on a regular basis.

Jazz is soothing and relaxing, yet very distinctive. Many single jazz aficionados are attractive, mature-minded, and creative. Appreciating jazz is definitely a worthwhile credential for a single prospect.

Lines for Jazz Clubs

❏ "Have you always been into jazz?"

❏ "Jazz is the best. It's so relaxing."

❏ "I've heard about an upcoming jazz festival. Have you ever been to one?"

❏ "Who are your favorite jazz recording artists?"

❏ "What do you think of this group?"

KARAOKE SING-ALONGS

Karaoke sing-alongs, which originated in Japan, are one of the most popular ways to get out and meet other singles. Before a sing-along gets under way, you are given a list of the song options. There are hundreds of songs to choose from. You check off your selections, then return the form to the disc jockey or Karaoke master of ceremonies. During the sing-along, when a song is selected for play, the words to the song appear on a giant screen and the background music—just the music, no vocals—begins to play. If you are one of the people who selected the song, then you are a singer! You sing the lyrics that are conveniently displayed on the screen.

Some establishments have the singing participants gather on the dance floor or stage; some let the participants sing from their seats. Try to scan the audience as soon as you arrive to see if there are any attractive prospects. And remember—location, location, location! You must be within striking distance of your prospect to make successful contact. No matter where your prospect is singing from—the dance floor, the stage, or his seat—you must be in close proximity. While you are singing, you can try to make eye contact and smile at your prospect. When the song is over, a conversation hopefully will ensue. If not, you can use an opening line to break the ice.

Karaoke sing-alongs are currently being featured at many nightclubs and restaurant bars throughout the country. For the businesses, Karaoke is generating a major flow of customer traffic and, therefore, increased profits. Meanwhile, for single people, it is another way to increase the odds of meeting a promising prospect.

Lines for Karaoke Sing-Alongs

❏ "Have you ever sung at one of these before?"

❏ "You have a wonderful singing voice. Are you a professional singer?"

❏ "Your voice is beautiful. Would you sing me a lullaby?"

❏ "What's your favorite song? I'd sing it, but then it probably wouldn't be your favorite any more!"

CONCLUSION

If you are serious about meeting someone, you need to use your evenings to their fullest. Attending cinema, music, and dance events will expose you to many interesting, artistic, and fun-loving people. So plan to spend a few nights each month at various entertainment events. While buying popcorn or boogying on the dance floor, you might meet your perfect match.

15

Local Spots—
Unexpected
Meeting Grounds

oesn't it seem like some of the most solid couples have met at the most unexpected of places? There are countless stories about chance encounters in health food stores, laundromats, local Chinese take-out restaurants, and church services. Wouldn't you like to have such a story to tell?

This chapter suggests that in the most ordinary places, you can locate the most extraordinary prospects. It's a matter of being willing and prepared to take advantage of every opportunity around you. Hopefully, you'll have a new perspective on everything from local libraries to international airports after reading the following sections. We hope to convince you even to look at professional office waiting rooms and long lines in facilities such as banks and post offices as possible meeting grounds!

HOUSES OF WORSHIP

Go to your chosen house of faith on your day of worship, and you might be amazed at all the single prospects you'll find. Many single people have some religious beliefs and enjoy attending church or synagogue. While you're being seated, or while the sermon is progressing, scan the congregation for attractive prospects. When you find someone whom you are attracted to, "lock on" to him with eye contact and a smile. You can make your initial move right after the service is over, or during an intermission period.

In addition to prayer services, many churches and synagogues are the settings for a variety of religious clubs, classes, and other activities. These functions are also ideal for meeting prospects. So if you're wait-

135

ing at home, praying to meet someone and getting no results, you should try your local church or synagogue. Your prayers just may be answered there.

Lines for Houses of Worship

❑ "My inner voice said that I should come to church/synagogue today, and I'm glad I listened."

❑ "You look like the answer to my prayers."

❑ "I honestly hope this is divine fate that I am lucky enough to meet you like this."

❑ "Do you know if this _____ has a singles club?" *(Insert house of worship.)*

LIBRARIES

The library is a marvelous place to meet someone new. You can start a conversation over any subject that you or your prospect may be reading about—just remember to speak softly. Some places where you can look for singles are among the stacks, at the worktables, by the magazine stands, and by the videotape racks. Many successful relationships have begun in libraries, with a love of reading or an interest in a specific subject as the common denominator.

Lines for Libraries

❑ "Could you help me look up something on the computer?"

❑ "Have you read any good books recently?"

❑ "Do you know if this library has a book club?"

❑ "I miss the card catalog! How about you?"

RESTAURANTS

Dining is considered to be one of our greatest pleasures. As such, places for dining are naturals as settings to meet and then develop relationships with interesting prospects. Dining out in restaurants is popular among single people. It's a fantastic way to meet other singles while at the same time enjoying a meal. Let's discuss different types of dining establishments and how to take advantage of them.

Pizza Parlors

If you like pizza (and even if you don't!), an ideal spot to find single prospects is your local pizza parlor. Since pizza is satisfying, quick, and easy, many singles go to local pizza parlors on a regular basis. Those who get their pizza delivered miss opportunities to meet attractive prospects who eat at the parlor to enjoy their pizza fresh from the oven. Even if you just pick up your pizza instead of having it delivered, you will have a chance to meet prospects.

Lines for Pizza Parlors

❏ "Come join me at my table for some pizza."

❏ "Can I pull up at your table? I'll bring the drinks."

❏ "I'm taking a poll. What's your favorite pizza topping?"

❏ "I would sacrifice my last slice of pepperoni to meet you."

Diners and Coffee Shops

Other eateries popular with singles are diners and coffee shops. These establishments fit in perfectly with the single lifestyle because they generally aren't fancy or expensive. They often have counters where you can sit down and eat your meal next to other singles. This is very conducive to starting an informal conversation. Also, because the diner/coffee shop atmosphere is down-home and friendly, starting a conversation with someone seated in a booth while you're standing, with someone standing while you're seated, or even between booth and counter is not that difficult.

You can find single prospects waiting in line to be seated, following the host or hostess to a seat, seated at the counter or in a booth, and waiting to pay their checks at the cashier's stand. Single prospects are everywhere in this type of restaurant, and it's up to you to meet them.

Lines for Diners and Coffee Shops

❏ "Do you have any suggestions on what to order? You look very trustworthy."

❏ "That looks wonderful. What are you having?"

❑ "You're sitting in my favorite seat at the counter/in my favorite booth. Did you slip the maitre d' some cash to get it?"

❑ "I love diner food. It's just like mom used to make—only without the nagging!"

❑ "The instant I saw you, my heart and the cheese on my sandwich both started to melt."

Fast Food Restaurants

Because of their fast-paced lifestyle, many singles grab a quick meal at their favorite fast food restaurant. To meet and connect with other singles at such establishments, you'll need to avoid the drive-through window and actually go into the restaurant. You can find single prospects standing in line, standing at the fixings bar, seated, and even working behind the counter.

Fast food restaurants are everywhere. The best time to meet other singles is at mealtime, but anytime is a good time.

Lines for Fast Food Restaurants

❑ "Can I do the fixings for you?"

❑ "Let me help you get all that stuff back to your table."

❑ "I'd like to recommend the roast duckling."

❑ "You look like a small fries/large fries/nonfries kind of person."

❑ "I've seen salad bars with less stuff than this fixings bar."

❑ "I'm afraid I'm going to have to issue you a citation for excess lettuce/onions/tomatoes/ketchup being dropped on the fixings table."

Fun Eateries

Fun eateries are popping up all over the country. The atmosphere is lighthearted, with music and interesting artifacts adorning the restaurant walls. The food is good, and it's served without much of a wait. There is also usually a bar, where you'll find plenty of singles loosening up with a drink before sitting down to their meal. Examples of this type of restaurant are the popular national chains TGI Fridays, Houlihans, Bennigans, Ground Round, and Fuddruckers. In addition, many local, privately owned fun eateries have probably already cropped up in your home town.

Check the restaurant guide in your local newspaper for a listing of these restaurants. Singles are attracted to fun eateries, so find out about all the places in your area. You'll be glad you made the effort.

Lines for Fun Eateries

❏ "Have you eaten here before? I come strictly for the frogs' legs. I've found that a cup of coffee plus an order of frogs' legs really gets me hopping through the rest of the day."

❏ "The sight of you warmed my heart and my cup of coffee."

❏ "Please join me at my table. I'll buff and shine the seat. I'll dust away any crumbs. Whatever it takes to make you feel comfortable."

❏ "I've been so anxious to meet you that I've actually been hoping you would start choking on food so that I could perform the Heimlich maneuver, save you, and introduce myself."

Specialty Restaurants

Specialty restaurants, such as Italian, Chinese, seafood, and gourmet eateries, are ideal places for singles to find prospects. Go into one of these restaurants with the right kind of attitude—a positive one—and chances are that you'll have a delightful meal plus meet someone special.

Lines for Specialty Restaurants

❏ "What's your favorite type of restaurant?"

❏ "Have you eaten here before?"

❏ "What's the specialty of the house?"

❏ "What's a nice girl/guy like you doing in a nice place like this without a nice guy/girl like me?"

Salad Bars

Salad bars are excellent spots to look for single prospects. You'll find singles busily filling their salad plates with a variety of different vegetables, fruits, and toppings. Many spend time contemplating what to add next; "salad loading" can be a major decision for some singles. Most people, however, visit the salad bar just briefly to fix up their salad and then go right back to their seat to eat it. Your mission here, should you decide to accept it, is to approach a prospect first and fill up your salad plate last. Take your salad plate and head directly over to an attractive prospect. You'll need to act quickly before your prospect is "salad loaded" and ready to return to her seat.

Lines for Salad Bars

❏ "Do you know what the different salad dressings are?"

❏ "That looks like a wonderful salad."

❏ "You scoop very neatly. I'm extremely impressed. Where did you learn how to scoop like that?"

❏ "How do you fill your salad plate without banging your head on this apparatus? I already have a mild concussion." *(This line is for use at salad bars with overhead lighting units or sneeze guards.)*

❏ "Every time I go to the salad bar, one of the restaurant staff has to clean up after me."

❏ "How did I get so lucky to find you in my salad bar line?"

❏ "I'll scoop veggies for you if you dip dressing for me. I took Scooping 101 in college."

❏ "Will you scoop for me while I hold my plate/hold my plate while I scoop? I can't walk and chew gum at the same time."

Quite a few types of eateries have been identified in this section. You should go out and try as many as possible. Notice where the hot spots are in your area and frequent them. Singles often return to good places with single friends!

STORES

Shopping is one of those activities that everyone must do at one time or another. But instead of letting it be a chore, why not make it pleasurable and productive? After all, you're not the only single person shopping—why not try to meet some prospects? Let's discuss some of the places where most people shop regularly and what you can do to meet other singles there.

Supermarkets

Shopping in a supermarket is a terrific way to meet prospects. You can scan the aisles for an attractive prospect and then, when the prospect strolls into your immediate vicinity, put on your most perplexed look and ask a contrived question about a product: "Do you know what the difference is between pea pods and peas?" "Do you know what shelf the canned unsweetened turnips are on?" It doesn't matter if your product question is genuine or ridiculously absurd. What matters is that you make contact.

Also, in a supermarket, if you get a smile or glance from a prospect, there are many aisles, in addition to the checkout counters, in which you can make follow-up contact. (Use the angled mirrors on the ceiling to keep track of your prospect's movements.) You could even make an effort to get in line behind the prospect. Then a conversation is likely to ensue.

Lines for Supermarkets

❏ "May I push your cart? I'm the local pusher."

❏ "Did you get everything on your shopping list?"

❏ "Excuse me, but I'd like to cite you for double-parking your shopping cart in aisle five."

❏ "Two thousand carts outside and I pick the one with a squeaky wheel. Do you have any oil on you?"

❏ "May I have the honor of double-bagging for you?"

❏ "Do you think we'll make it to the front of the line while we still have a few good years left?"

❏ "Thank you for your road courtesy. You're a good driver." *(This line is for use with a prospect who has moved his or her shopping cart in some way to let you pass.)*

❏ "Decisions, decisions—should I choose the long checkout line with the light loads, or should I go with the short line of heavy loads? Why is life so troubling?"

❏ "Please, no speeding. We use radar to catch speeders in these aisles."
(This line is for use with a prospect who is moving briskly down the aisle with a shopping cart.)

Health Food Stores

Health food stores are great places to meet attractive, health-conscious prospects. Many singles spend their spare time working out to get and stay in optimum shape. These singles tend to shop at health food stores for protein or diet shakes, vitamin supplements, cruelty-free cosmetics, and healthy foods. People who shop in health food stores care about their health and about the environment. What better quality could you want in a prospect than respect for good health and for the Earth?

Lines for Health Food Stores

❏ "Do you know if I can get organic vegetables or fruit here?"

❏ "I'm looking for an effective weight-loss product. What do you use to stay so trim?"

❏ "Is this the only health food store in the area, or are there others?"

❏ "What vitamins do you take to look so healthy?"

❏ "You must take a lot of vitamins to look that beautiful/handsome."

Farmers Markets

Farmers markets frequently house many different vendors under one roof. You're likely to find singles meandering about searching for fresh vegetables, fruit, bread, pastries, meat, fish, gourmet snacks, and flowers. Most farmers markets allow only vendors who carry fresh, high quality products. Stop in at a local farmers market and treat your palate to some new taste sensations. And treat your eyes to some fine-looking prospects, too!

Lines for Farmers Markets

❏ "Is the produce fresh today?"

❏ "I just love fresh fruits and vegetables. How about you?"

❏ "When I see these fresh foods, I just want to go out and grow them myself. Do you garden?"

Malls and Department Stores

Shopping malls are excellent places to meet prospects. Malls are loaded with single people out spending money or just window-shopping. Prospects can be found walking in and out of stores, browsing, snacking in the food court, or sitting on benches relaxing. Just be casual, friendly, and sincere in your approach. Remember, there's no reason you can't buy a pair of shoes on sale plus meet a prospect in the same afternoon.

Department stores are another good source of single people. You've got a lot of prospects browsing through the various departments, while more are working throughout the store. Go department-store shopping before or after any major holiday for a prospecting bonanza. Some astute singles are already aware of this prospecting treasure, and now you can join their ranks.

Lines for Shopping Malls

❏ "What's your favorite store in this mall?"

❏ "Are there any good sales here today?"

❏ "I want you to know that you've been the best part of my shopping experience."

❏ "If you're wondering whether to buy that, let me say that you'd look wonderful in it." *(This line is for use when a prospect is clothes shopping.)*

❏ "So, what are you buying for me? You don't have to keep it a secret. You can tell me now."

❏ "Does this place have a lost and found? I'm looking for a gift." *(This line should be said with obvious humor.)*

❏ "How does this look on me?"

❏ "What do you think of this as a gift for my _____?" *(Insert name of friend or relative.)*

❏ "Do you know where to find men's clothing/customer service/the elevator?"

❏ "Can I ask what perfume/cologne you're wearing? I'm looking to get a gift for my _____."

❏ "I'm clothing challenged. Since you are definitely not, can you help me select a _____?"

❏ "I know this seems odd, but you look like you have great taste. Can you help me find a _____?"

❏ "Do you know if there's a bookstore/jewelry store in this mall?"

Automotive Stores

Probably the best specialty store a woman could "shop at" to meet single men is an automotive store. Many single men spend hours working on their cars, or fixing up old cars, as a hobby. They will be impressed by a woman looking at distributor caps or even just at steering wheel covers. Most will be more than happy to answer any questions.

Look for prospects entering or leaving the store, browsing in the aisles, milling in front of the store, or working behind the counters. Just have some knowledge about the auto part you're supposedly looking for. You may end up leaving the store with a car accessory *and* a date for Friday night.

Lines for Automotive Stores

❏ "Could you recommend a gift for my father's birthday? He loves cars."

❏ "Could you recommend a good alarm system for my car?"

❏ "I need new windshield wipers for my car. Are they difficult to install? Do you know how to put them on?"

❏ "I'm feeling lucky. Do you know where I can find fuzzy dice?"

❏ "Do you know if they sell car horns here?"

Flea Markets

Flea markets are always great places for meeting prospects. Most people are happy and at ease there, making it a good environment to strike up a conversation. A little eye contact, a smile, and you're on your way. Conversation can be started easily over interests such as antiques and collectibles. You can converse about how ecstatic you are not having to be at work, or about how you really like finding great bargains. Whatever comes to mind to begin a friendly conversation is enough to initiate contact. Then offer to treat your new acquaintance to lunch, an ice-cream cone, or a cup of coffee.

Lines for Flea Markets

❏ "I shop here regularly. How come I haven't seen you before?"

❏ "The only part about shopping that I hate is carrying all those heavy bags from the car into the house."

❏ "I hope you've found what you were looking for."

If the answer is no: "Well, then let me be of assistance to you."

If the answer is yes: "You must be a good shopper. Maybe you could help me find what I'm looking for."

Yard and House Sales

Many homeowners and apartment dwellers sell unwanted belongings at advertised yard or house sales. Singles looking to furnish or accessorize their houses or apartments inexpensively often shop at these events for bargains. You can, too, but keep your eyes open for appealing prospects as well.

Lines for Yard and House Sales

❏ "Do you think this table could be successfully stripped and stained?"

❏ "Look at this! Do you think it could be worth something?"

Card Shops

How can card shops be helpful to you? In some busy ones, you'll find prospects chuckling over card selections up and down the aisles. Once you spot an attractive prospect, position yourself near her and act like you're looking for a card. It will be much easier to strike up a conversation if you're both looking at the same kind of cards. With a little luck, you will need to return to the card shop to buy an affection card for your newfound friend.

Lines for Card Shops

❏ "What do you think of this card for my friend/sister/father?"

❏ "Do you like funny cards, or do you prefer the more serious ones?"

❏ "Excuse me, but can I help you find a card? I don't work here, but I'd just love to help you."

Bookstores and Music Stores

Other shops where singles abound are bookstores and music stores. People love reading, and you are apt to find a lot of prospects standing in the aisles browsing through books. The best time to scan bookstores for single prospects is on weekends, as most people are off from work, and in the evenings, when many single prospects read and write in the café areas. With the advent of mega-bookstores such as Borders or Barnes and Noble, which feature chic espresso bars, more and more singles can be found meandering through the aisles or sipping cappuccino on weekdays, too.

Music stores are also popular with singles. Look in the section featuring the type of music you prefer, and you'll have a ready-made shared interest. But if the prospect is really appealing to you, forget the music—just hum a hello. You can take turns with the stereo, when the time comes.

Lines for Bookstores and Music Stores

❑ "Do you know where the _____ are?" *(Insert type of book or CD.)*

❑ "Can you tell me where I can find _____?" *(Insert name of book or CD.)*

❑ "What kind of books/music do you like?"

❑ "What do you think of this book/CD?"

Video/DVD Stores

Considering the cost and effort involved in going out to the movies, many singles are finding it much simpler and cheaper to rent a movie and watch it at home. If your town or neighborhood has one of the big chain video/DVD stores such as West Coast Video or Blockbuster Video, the odds will be better that you'll meet prospects. After all, these stores usually have a larger selection of movie titles and more copies of each title to enable them to service a more substantial clientele. If a small video/DVD store is all that you have, however, so be it; single people go there, too. You can find prospects wandering about the different aisles deciding which movies to rent or at the service counter renting or returning tapes.

Lines for Video Stores

❏ "I don't know about you, but I can't find anything I want to rent here. Do you want to go see a movie?"

❏ "I'm looking for a good comedy/thriller/mystery. Have you seen any good ones you could recommend?"

❏ "Do you like to watch movies in widescreen format?"

As you consider all the different types of stores, remember to look not only for prospects browsing and purchasing but for those working—cashiers, for example. Every store has a cashier. So, the next time you reach into your wallet to pay for something, you may also have a chance to walk away with a date for lunch or a movie. Let's close this section on stores, then, with a couple of lines to use on the employees of your favorite store.

Lines for Cashiers

❏ "You impress me with the way you handle money. What do you think about mutual funds?"

❏ "Could you please try to keep the total down for me?" *(This line often works very well. Since a product costs what it costs, the cashier will usually chuckle.)*

❏ "Don't forget my ten-percent senior citizen's discount." *(This line works well when you're anything but a senior citizen and your prospect knows it.)*

❏ "Price check—aisle four! I don't know why—maybe I need to be committed to an institution—but I've always wanted to say that in a checkout line."

LAUNDROMATS

Another place to meet single prospects is, strange as it may seem, the laundromat. Many singles live in apartments or houses that don't have washers or dryers. They therefore spend at least some time every week, usually on Saturday or Sunday, in the laundromat. While their clothes are rinsing and spin drying, these singles usually read a book or magazine out of boredom.

Laundromats offer various opportunities to begin a conversation. Break the ice with a prospect while loading or unloading your clothes, adding detergent or fabric softener to your washer, getting quarters from the change machine, or simply waiting for your machine to finish. Many laundromats now have televisions for the patrons to watch while waiting; these provide many topics to help start conversations. Some laundromats even feature "singles nights," where you'll find music, dancing, beer, food, roses, and a hostess to coordinate different activities. "Singles nights" are usually held by savvy entrepreneurs on the slowest night of the week. Of course, there will still be loads of singles with piles of dirty clothes to be washed on any night of the week! Whichever way you look at it, if you use laundromats to do your wash, you should seriously consider the potential of meeting prospects there.

Lines for Laundromats

❏ "What are the advantages of your detergent over mine?"

❏ "Can I give you a hand with that load?"

❏ "Which machines would you recommend?"

❏ "Would you care to take a spin during the spin cycle?"

❏ "I've been thinking about trying your detergent. Have you ever used mine?"

❏ "Can I get you some more change while you load your washer/dryer?"

❏ "I found this sock on the floor. Is it yours?"

❏ "Could I borrow a cup of bleach/a dryer sheet?"

❏ "Would you like some help folding your clothes?"

❏ "Would you like to go for a _____ during the drying cycle?" *(Insert appropriate beverage.)*

❏ "I've never used fabric softener. Is it really worth using?"

❏ "I feel like I've aged ten years while waiting for my clothes to dry."

❏ "When I came in here to wash my clothes, I was cleanly shaved—and look at me now." *(This line is for use by a man with whiskers.)*

❏ "I've got two dryers here, but I only need one. Would you like to use the second?"

PUBLIC TRANSPORTATION

People have to travel. And what's wrong with trying to strike up a conversation with someone interesting while you're getting from one place to another? One of the reasons travel is so conducive to meeting prospects is that, for a period of time, you and your fellow travelers are confined to the vehicle of transportation. There are some people who are so successful at meeting prospects while traveling that they go on short bus or train trips specifically for the purpose. At their destination, they just turn around and go right back home again. So, consider using your transit time to approach interesting prospects the next time you have to use public transportation.

Trains and Buses

Many singles use the bus or train on a daily basis to commute to work or school. Chances are that if you are one of these people, you see attractive prospects every day. You don't need to be a regular commuter, however, to take advantage of the opportunities on the train or bus. If you need to travel for any reason, keep your eyes and ears open. You can make contact in the ticket office, on the platform while waiting for your train or bus, on the train or bus, or even when leaving the train or bus. In addition, if you're waiting for a friend or relative to arrive, be sure to scan the platform and pick a good spot to do your waiting in.

Lines for Trains and Buses

❏ "Would you join me for the ride to work/home?"

❏ "I don't know what it is, but whenever I have an important meeting/a must-make appointment/a crucial exam, the train/bus is invariably late."

❏ "That looks like an interesting book. What's it about?"

❏ "Can I buy you a(n)_____ while we wait?" (*Insert appropriate beverage.*)

❏ "I've been taking this train/bus to work/school for a long time, and I can't believe I've never seen you."

Airplanes and Airports

Airplanes and airports also offer great opportunities to meet other singles. People take planes for business reasons, for vacations, or to visit friends or relatives. Single prospects can be found working on the plane or in the terminal, standing in line at the check-in counter, killing time in the gift shop or restaurant, waiting at the gate, sitting on the plane, waiting for their luggage in the baggage claim area, or waiting for a taxi, limo, or shuttlebus. Also watch for singles who are waiting for or dropping off a traveler. The opportunities abound at the airport or on a plane. So the next time someone asks you for a lift to the airport, say yes.

Lines for Airplanes and Airports

❏ "Would you like some help carrying your luggage?"

❏ "The instant I saw you, I realized it wasn't important if I was departing or arriving. I only wanted to meet this lovely/handsome person."

❏ "You even look good with an oxygen mask over your face." (*This line is for use with the flight attendant after she demonstrates how to use the oxygen mask.*)

❏ "Excuse me. Are you a (*name of airline*) flight attendant? I'm flying (name of airline), and I hope the attendants on my flight look as good as you."

❏ "I want to thank the ticket agent. She promised me that there would be a strikingly beautiful person on this flight, and she didn't lie."

You probably never dreamed of meeting your soul mate at the lockers of bus stations or standing at an airport vending machine. But strange and wonderful things have been known to happen at these spots. Because of the volume and variation of people at public transportation locations, you have a great chance to meet some interesting prospects while traveling from point A to point B.

PROFESSIONAL OFFICE WAITING ROOMS

As strange as it may seem, you can meet prospects while waiting to see your doctor, dentist, lawyer, or other professional. It's true that some people in waiting rooms sit with their heads down, waiting (hopefully, fearfully) for their name to be called. But there are other people who, to make the time go by, are very willing to make conversation. If you keep a smile on your face and make eye contact with other clients, you will invite them to relax and open up. You may find yourself in a profound conversation within minutes.

Lines for Professional Office Waiting Rooms

❏ "Have you been waiting here long?"

❏ "What have you heard about this _____?" (*Insert appropriate type of professional.*)

❏ "When I first showed up for my appointment, I was fourteen years old!"

❏ "Isn't this a beautiful/noisy/interesting waiting room?"

❏ "You have the most beautiful eye." (*This humorous line is for use in an optometrist's or optician's waiting room.*)

LONG LINES

Any time you have to stand on a long line—for example, at the Department of Motor Vehicles, the post office, or the bank—look at it as a great, although unusual, place to meet singles. People tend to respond more willingly to opening lines or questions when they're waiting on line. After all, while waiting on line, there isn't very much to do except chitchat. So, when you are ready to get on line, look around first. If your timing is good, you can position yourself directly behind a good prospect on the same line or beside one on the next line. Then don't wait; make your move!

Lines for Long Lines

❏ "How long have you been waiting?"

❏ "What type of car do you drive?" (*This line is for use at the Department of Motor Vehicles.*)

❏ "Is this where I get a license for my horse?" (*This line is for use at the Department of Motor Vehicles.*)

❏ "I hope this bank doesn't run out of money by the time we get up to a teller!"

❏ "My license/registration will expire by the time I get up to the counter."

❏ "If they had to pay us to wait in line, we'd be out of here a lot faster!"

CONCLUSION

Upon completing this chapter, you have also completed Part II. Now you have a plethora of places where you can scope out prospects and make your move. Even if you are not the type to join singles services, clubs, sports teams, or community groups, you certainly have gathered a few ideas by now. After all, this chapter highlights many of the places that you visit weekly. Perhaps you just didn't think to look for prospects at your post office or pizza parlor. Your favorite local spots will seem very different to you now! All it takes is awareness and energy. Now get to it!

A Bright New Beginning

*Y*ou might not yet have achieved as much success in your love life as you would like. But you have not allowed yourself to be defeated. You decided to learn some additional skills and strategies in order to improve your ability to meet people and develop lasting relationships. You have gathered new insights and refreshed your motivation, which will certainly benefit your quest for a wonderful relationship. You are determined to change the direction of your social life.

Now that you've finished reading this book, don't put it away. Don't feel that its fate is to collect dust on a shelf. Use this book as a resource. Any time you plan on doing anything to meet people, and any time you decide to try a new or different activity, thumb through this book for some helpful hints. You may find that each time you go through the book, you pick up a new idea—one you missed during your last review simply because it did not fit with what you were aiming to accomplish at that particular time. Turn to this book, as well, if you are feeling discouraged and need a little support.

DON'T LET REJECTION STOP YOU

Remember that in any quest to develop a romantic relationship, rejection is part of the process. If you join a singles activity expecting 100 percent success, you're bound to be disappointed. Do you know *anyone* who has never experienced ups and downs in his quest for the perfect relationship? We don't. Everyone experiences the unpleasantness of rejection.

If you are shot down, you can look at it in a number of different ways. You can take it as a personal affront, feel two-feet tall, and decide that you're never going to try to meet someone again! Or you can try to figure out what happened to cause the rejection, so that you can learn from it. Which do you think is the better option?

There are many reasons why a person may not to be interested in you. Keep something in mind: If somebody rejects you, it is not you as a person that is being rejected. Does the prospect really know you from just one preliminary meeting? Of course not. What this person really is rejecting is either something about your presentation, something about your approach, or something in himself that he cannot deal with at the present time.

Do you like everybody you meet? Would you respond favorably to every person who approached to you? Probably not. So therefore, how can you expect each person you encounter to respond favorably to you? If someone rejects you, remind yourself that you, too, are not drawn to every available single. Then pull yourself together and move on.

Rejection should not be a deterrent. In fact, it can strengthen your character, as well as your techniques, so look at the positive side. Any time an attempt to meet someone does not work out the way you would like, ask yourself what you could have done better—how you could have improved your approach, how you could have delivered your lines better, how you could have presented yourself more confidently, and so on. Practice makes you better, so keep practicing your lines, your follow-up conversation, and the way you present yourself. Every bit of knowledge you gain from an experience will help you in subsequent attempts.

If you find that you're still having difficulty, watch other people. Look around you, pick out the people who seem to be successful a great portion of the time, and watch carefully what they do. Or ask people how they like to be approached. You can use everything you learn.

PURSUE MORE INFORMATION

Let's say you feel that some of the locations and functions suggested in Part II are great for you. However, you're wondering how to find such clubs, organizations, and resources in your area, in order to put the suggestions into action. The best place to start is the Singles Calendar of Events column in your local newspaper, if it has one. Also, on certain days of the week, many newspapers feature a special section that offers a sort of "What's Happening," "Upcoming Events," "Things to Do," or "Weekend Activities" roundup. Often, listings of singles activities are included. Almost every location and function you read about in this book will be mentioned at some time. Also, read magazines in your areas of interest, since they, too, may have columns or advertisements describing singles functions or special events.

In addition, check with local health, civic, and community organizations, which frequently have information on what regular activities are locally available and what special events are coming up. Local libraries also have a wealth of information that will help you decide what to do and when.

And, of course, you can speak to other singles to find out what they are doing. Not only will you get details about what opportunities exist and how you can get involved, but just asking for information is a great opening gambit to meet prospects.

LET US KNOW HOW YOU DO

Although we may never meet face to face, we feel that we have interacted with you through the pages of this book. We would like to know how our techniques, tips, ideas, and suggestions have worked for you. Therefore, we welcome letters from you in which you tell us your success stories. Write to us in care of Square One Publishers, 115 Herricks Road, Garden City Park, New York 11040. Tell us what line worked for you. What singles venues did you find most helpful? What suggested locations worked for you? In addition, let us know what areas you'd like to learn more about. What situations are still difficult for you? Keep us informed. We may be able to use your input in a future publication.

As a matter of fact, we just may have provided you with the best ice-breaking approach of all. Why not use our request for feedback as a clever way to initiate conversations with prospects. You can say, "Excuse me. I'm trying to help out someone who is gathering information for a book. The book is on lines and approaches to use for breaking the ice· when meeting someone new. Can you help?" And don't forget to send us the responses!

It's now time to put what you've learned to good use. Walk tall, be proud, and have fun meeting people. No better cliché can be used for closing this book than to wish you what you wish for yourself!

About
the Authors

Larry Glanz is a relationships expert. With a successful sales management background, Mr. Glanz quickly learned the importance of effective selling techniques in overcoming objections and winning over prospective clients. For more than twenty years, he has studied and analyzed the mating customs of singles in the United States. By applying his most successful sales tactics to the art of developing relationships, he has created many highly effective relationship-building strategies—from icebreakers to date-makers. He currently lives in suburban Philadelphia with his wife and three sons.

Robert H. Phillips, Ph.D., is a practicing psychologist on Long Island, New York. He is the founder and director of the Center for Coping, a multi-service organization offering private and group counseling to help individuals cope with a variety of situations.

The author of twenty-five books on how to deal with various chronic health conditions, Dr. Phillips has also written numerous articles on a variety of subjects in the field of psychology. He is the coauthor of the bestseller *Love Tactics*. He has lectured at conventions, universities, and professional meetings throughout the country, and has appeared on local and national radio and television programs. Currently he is the host of a weekly radio show on Long Island, New York.

Index

FALLING IN LOVE AGAIN

The Mature Woman's Guide to Finding Romantic Fulfillment

Monica Morris, PhD

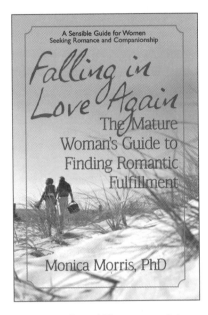

Statistics point to the fact that more and more older singles are dating and getting married. If you find yourself in the category of older single but not part of this statistic, don't fret. Help is on its way in the form of a new and unique book: *Falling in Love Again.* Social psychology expert Dr. Monica Morris has created an empowering resource for the millions of women in her age group looking for romance and companionship. Not only does Dr. Morris draw upon her skills as a social scientist, she draws from her experience as a woman who found herself unexpectedly single—and clueless—later in life.

The book begins by first exploring a woman's expectations of finding love—preparing her for the real world. It then looks at her need for self-assurance and poise, offering numerous ways to bolster her self-esteem. From there, the book provides dozens of sensible suggestions on finding that special someone—from personal ads to online dating to matchmaking services. It includes such important details as costs, accessibility, and precautions. It then addresses the more intimate questions regarding sex, living together, personal needs, and independence. In addition, at the end of the book, there is a unique resource of services, websites, and organizations designed to help women find a significant other—or just to have fun.

For the millions of women who find themselves in a very different and lonely place later in their lives, *Falling in Love Again* can help them discover that there is life after loneliness. The practical and compassionate advice found in *Falling in Love Again* can truly make it happen.

About the Author

Monica Morris has an MA and PhD in Sociology from the University of Southern California. Her areas of expertise include social psychology, sociology of the emotion, and medical sociology. She was a professor of sociology in the California State University System for over twenty years. She has had several sociology works published. She resides with her husband in Southern California.

$14.95 • 224 pages • 6 x 9-inch quality paperback • Relationships / Love & Romance • ISBN: 0-7570-0136-X

OUR SECRET RULES

Why We Do the Things We Do

Jordan Weiss, MD

We all live our lives according to a set of rules that regulate our behaviors. Some rules are quite clear. These are conscious beliefs we hold dear. Others, however, are unconscious. These are our secret rules, and when we do things that go against them, we experience stress, anxiety, apprehension, and emotional exhaustion—and we never know why. That is, until now. In *Our Secret Rules,* Dr. Jordan Weiss offers a unique system that helps uncover our most secret rules.

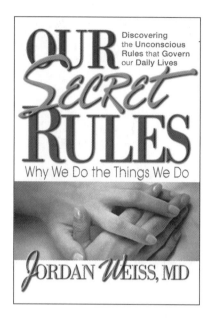

The book begins by explaining the important roles that conscious and unconscious rules play in our daily existence. Each chapter focuses on a key area of our lives—money, religion, gender identification, work, friendships, health, power, personal expression, marriage, and sex. Within each chapter, there are challenging questions for the reader. The answers provide a personal look at how we are likely to behave when faced with specific situations. Each chapter ends with an analysis of potential answers that is designed to reveal the extent of our secret rules.

Our Secret Rules concludes by explaining how we can use our newly gained insights to improve the way we feel about ourselves and others. For once we are aware of our rules, we can then learn to live within their boundaries, or we can attempt to change them. And as we do, we can enjoy the benefits of happier, more harmonious lives.

About the Author

Dr. Jordan Weiss received his medical degree from the University of Illinois Medical School in Chicago. With an emphasis on the body-mind-spirit connection, he has worked at several leading complementary medical centers. A practicing psychiatrist for over twenty years, Dr. Weiss currently works at Irvine's Center for Psychoenergetic Therapy in California. He is the author of several published articles on emotional responses, and is a highly regarded speaker.

$11.95 • 184 pages • 6 x 9-inch quality paperback • Self-Help/Psychology • ISBN 0-7570-0010-X

12 MAGIC WANDS

The Art of Meeting Life's Challenges

G.G. Bolich, PhD

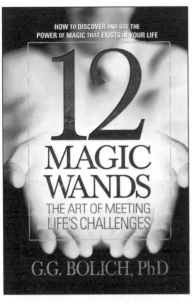

Magic exists. It is everywhere. It surrounds us and infuses us. It holds the power to transform us. It isn't always easy to see, but then again, it wouldn't be magic if it was. Counselor and educator G.G. Bolich has written *Twelve Magic Wands*—a unique and insightful guide for recognizing the magic in our lives, and then using it to improve our physical, mental, and spiritual selves. It provides a step-by-step program that empowers the reader to meet and conquer life's consistent challenges.

The book begins by explaining what magic is and where it abides. It then offers twelve magic "wands" that can transform one's life for the better. Each wand provides practical tools and exercises to gain control over a specific area, such as friendship and love. Throughout the book, the author presents inspiring true stories of people who have used the magic in their lives to both help themselves and point the way to others.

The world can be a difficult place. Loneliness, disappointments, tragedies, and dead ends can sometimes seem insurmountable. Losing the magic in one's life can make it even more difficult. *Twelve Magic Wands* provides real ways to make it better—first inside, and then out.

About the Author

Dr. G.G. Bolich received his Master's of Divinity from George Fox University in Newberg, Oregon. He earned his first PhD in educational leadership from Gonzaga University in Spokane, Washington, and a second in psychology from The Union Institute in Cincinnati, Ohio. Currently a professor at Webster University in South Carolina, Dr. Bolich has taught courses at the university level since 1975. He also provides private counseling, specializing in trauma resolution, and is the published author of six titles and numerous articles in the fields of psychology, religion, and spirituality. Among his published works are *Psyche's Child, Introduction to Religion,* and *The Christian Scholar.*

$15.95 • 160 pages • 6 x 9-inch quality paperback • Self-Help/Mind, Body, Spirit • ISBN 0-7570-0086-X

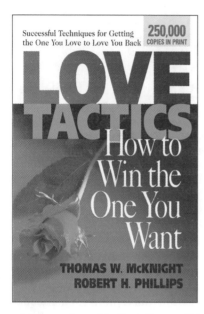

Successful Techniques for Getting the One You Love to Love You Back — **250,000 COPIES IN PRINT**

LOVE TACTICS

How to Win the One You Want

Thomas W. McKnight and Robert H. Phillips

Maybe that very special someone is not as far out of reach as you think. Maybe what you need are a few effective strategies to finally make the right moves. Even if you're very shy, a little on the quiet side, or simply not the social success you'd like to be, *Love Tactics* may have the answers you've been looking for.

Divided into two sections, *Love Tactics* presents dozens of strategic techniques that are designed to help you in the most exciting search-and-succeed activities of your life. These strategies, which are found in Part One, will help you win the love of that special someone. With each tactic, you'll find yourself becoming more enthusiastic, confident, and eager to approach the person of your dreams in an effort to win his or her love. For those who have already found a romantic partner, but have lost or are in danger of losing that person, Part Two presents tactics for winning back a lost love.

Written in a warm, easy-going style, this book offers a wealth of practical advice on how to get the one you love to love you back. You don't have to settle for anything (or anyone) less. The dream is in sight—and *Love Tactics* is all you need to make that dream a reality.

About the Authors

Thomas W. McKnight is a relationships expert. His columns on meeting the right person have appeared in leading U.S. singles newspapers and magazines over the past fifteen years. He has conducted dozens of relationship workshops throughout the country, and has also appeared on numerous radio and television shows, including Oprah.

Robert H. Phillips is a practicing psychologist and the director of the Center for Coping located in Westbury, New York. He is also the best-selling author of eight books dealing with various chronic health conditions, including *Coping With Lupus* and *Coping With Osteoarthritis*.

$12.95 • 208 pages • 6 x 9-inch paperback • Relationships/Love & Romance • ISBN 0-7570-0037-1

**For more information about our books,
visit our website at www.squareonepublishers.com.**